Белой Горячки

Галлюцинации очень
возможны.

Brain Fever #4

Publisher
Gene Yu

Editor
Mike Goodman

Produced quarterly by
Matchlock Press
PO Box 90606
Brooklyn, NY 11209

Correspondence
Write to us c/o Matchlock Press, or
email brainfever@matchlock.com.

Contents

2 / *Editorial*

3 / *Rockefeller Center* / Agir

4 / *White Privilege* / Mike Goodman

16 / *The Trial of Lickey Louse* / Vava

20 / *Colloquium At the End of the World* / Anicula

40 / *Magazine Ad From Outer Space* / Agir

41 / *Eve's Temptation* / Agir

49 / *Find-Your-Center(fold)* / Vava

52 / *Why We Occupy* / Olivia Schanzer

65 / *Subway Sketchbook* / Agir

74 / *To Land a Man* / Olivia Schanzer

85 / *Spectrum* / Agir

101 / *IBM Building Atrium* / Agir

102 / *Ballpoint Perps* / Vava

EDITORIAL

My friend,

Whatever faith tradition you've got—or if you don't have a shred of belief at all—spring is the time when all that lives, & croaks, & does its thing, recapitulates their beautiful existence by making love and making babies. But that's faith in the future, right there, when people do it. For us hairless apes, it ain't just rutting.

This is the time we build our nests, and open up our doors, go outside into the sunshine and check on our neighbors: Hey, man, how'd the winter serve you?

If we made it through the winter. But that's not all of us. Some people's daughters and sons didn't make it through. & the joy of their heart didn't make it through. We've got a nation of beautiful children who are very upset with us, & they have every right to be. & if you've made a child, you owe it to the future to not back out on that faith just yet. Yeah, you owe those kids something.

I don't care if the trees are blooming, we've got to bow our heads. Let's do it like us Jews do right about now at the Passover celebration, when we pour out the drops of wine from our cups for the plagues upon Egypt:

For America's dead, the holy souls of children. When we let you die we shoot down heaven. For all the kids who are lost in war, all over the world, & all their moms and dads too. For this generation of kids all around the world who have grown up without no vitamins, without no schooling, because of war. For those men & women who are carried away over borders breaking up their families because some fucker believed in borders— & there are no real fucking borders but the ones con men draw up. For our beautiful Earth, she's got a plastic field the size of France in the middle of the Pacific Ocean. For our beautiful mother, Earth, who keeps getting fracked. For all those who lost their lease & found themselves on the street. & every fucker who didn't eat dinner so that their kid could eat dinner. For the last male white rhinocerous who died, leaving his two widows, and made an end to that species.

It doesn't seem like there'll be anything left in the cup, when we pour all that out, but that last sip is still there. It's for you to drink.

I toast you now:

To life, as always!

Much love,
Mike

WHITE

PRIVILEGE

A Reminiscence
by Mike Goodman

Y OU want to know how I know about white privilege? Sometime in the early seventies I had a friend with a plan to transport a camper van full of dope over the border. The kind of situation where they hollowed out the walls and made room for bales of dope. My friend Jorge was a dark-skinned Mexican brother—really beautiful poet and an all-around good guy, as well—and because of that, coupled with his long hair, he had issues with the cops on both sides of the line. Though he was a naturalized American citizen and voted in every election that came up, even city council, he looked like an Indian. I think he told me he was of Aztec stock, or something along the lines. Had three or four x's in his last name, which tells it. He came from shamans, and what he told me about that would be enough for a story, and a good one.

Jorge wanted to lay low a bit, due to some issues he had had with the cops, but he had a business to run and he couldn't take sick leave. Besides, his wife was expecting their first baby, and they had bassinets to buy, and diapers, and the rest of that jazz.

Jorge asked me would I do it, and I hemmed and hawed a little. But the cut, man! Despite my reasonable fears and worries, I said yes. This was a situation where, if I took the gig, I wouldn't have to work for about a year. Not one class to teach, or white-collar hustle to grind out. Nothing, and the bills would still get paid, and

I could drink wine and eat red meat to my heart's content. No more Cheerios. No more beans and rice. I could go to the movies. Buy good-quality coffee beans. I had a novel in mind that I had been meaning to write for quite some time, and the idea that I might get that done! The inspiration on it was starting to get moldy, and still I only had some notes and afternoon dreaming.

Jorge—beautiful brother that he was—did not waste one breath reassuring me about the risk. I'm not, nor was I, a stupid man. Fuck. I could imagine Mexican cops prying open the van with crowbars just as well as the next. Me on the side of the road in cuffs, then bye-bye to the rest of my life. US wouldn't even notice I was gone, and what's going to happen to some hippie gringo in a Mexican prison? You've got an imagination for that, I'll bet!

Jorge's plan for me was that I would shave my beard and DA my hair like it was 1957 and I was captain of the football team. He even bought me pomade! I would sit out in the sun like that for several days so there would be no bikini line on my face. No sense that I'd ever been as disreputable as to have had a beard, you dig? Kind of how the terrorists do it, as I've read. You don't want to look like you were a head a few days before. Nor a jihadi motherfucker!

The next part was that he would find me a very blonde wife—some lovely little hippie lady, preferably with a kid or two—and the chick would dye her hair a few shades lighter then it was already—not cheap, just as Caucasian as she could get—and she would get it done up in a bouffant, really spray and tease it at an honest-to-God beauty parlor, such as none of us had stepped into in years, and put on a Jackie O-style dress and have her nails done. The whole trip of middle-American womanhood. Wedding ring, too, and make sure to wear a brassière, girl. The kids and mom got up in Peck & Peck. Wash out the knots from their wild hippie hair, give them a two-day crash course in mainstream socialization. Yes, ma'am.

They were going to make us a couple of driver's licenses, laminated and super-pretty. Whatever paperwork we needed. Jorge assured me they had some terrific forger they'd sprung out of prison for the job. Being a poet he was an ace fabulist. Later on it seemed to be clear bullshit, but we'll get to that!

I was introduced to Marcy and her girls in a village just over the border. We met at a taqueria where the owner was Jorge's cousin. All-right gent with a beatnik goatee and a little felt hat. I got the feeling right off that he was a poet, too, and when I asked him about it, he went to the back and got me a copy of his chapbook, *Los Espinas*, and took some money for it. I still have it. Nice print job in red and black.

Jorge made the introductions and ordered us lunch. He read us a poem in Spanish, which he said he composed about our journey. I didn't understand it at all, but Jorge had a really sonorous voice and I always enjoyed listening to him.

Marcy certainly looked the part already. She had on this yellow mini-dress and matching little shoes, under-fed but kind of in that Mia Farrow way, and the kids were wearing little clean rompers and had their hair in pony-tails, just like they stepped out of New Canaan! They were little blonde girls, such as my loins could not have issued, but they say now that in every child one half of the DNA wins out and takes dominance, so maybe that might have been the case here, if someone was going to bother to consider. Certainly my own Hebraic children look nothing like these two did. You look close at some Jews and consider the places we might have stopped off on our wanderings from Zion.

But when this pretty blond young woman opened her mouth! You knew right off that she hadn't stayed a night in New Canaan! She talked chakras and signs and doses, weed, UFOs, JFK, meridians and electromagnetics! She had that slow drawl of someone a little too burned out. Her eyes barely seemed to focus, and she took long pauses before answering your questions. The worst burnt-out New Yorkers never come close to sounding like that. NYC burn-outs still motormouth about politics and literature. It's just that the words stop making any fucking sense at all!

She offered me weed, pills, a sip

from her flask, and a hit of acid within five minutes of meeting me. I got a little scared faced with that. She could not take the hint when I told her nicely to get her shit together. I said it as clearly as I could: "Lady, I don't know you, but this is something serious. We've got to get it together and just scrub up, okay? We've got to look like a couple of beer-sipping straights, okay? You and me, old married couple. We don't even get laid anymore." She didn't have any sense of humor left in her, but she quit it with the offers. It didn't stop her from digging around in her purse, chewing on this and that. I couldn't help but worry. Not all hippie girls are created equal, and it figures that the one who's got your life in her hands is dosing just before you've got to do this dangerous thing.

The kids were even worse. They were those kind of commune kids who are always mewling and pulling on grown-ups' pant legs and having a tantrum every time you turn away. They looked clean at this moment, but you could tell that their natural habitat was crawling around in the dust without diapers. In fact, it seemed that at any moment they would burst out of their rompers and go back to their natural state. The baby certainly was not comfortable with clothes, and kept pulling at her straps to try to get the suit off. At this point I'm already sweating. I had a beer at lunch. I had another.

At a certain point I noticed what they were doing trying to get their rompers off, and tried to stop them. The little one bit my finger hard. I mean, like, the big baby teeth at the front really ripped open my skin. Human saliva is the most unclean, poisonous substance. There wasn't even clean water to wash it out there, so I just poured some beer on it. That shit stung! The mother did not care. Made no apologies at all, and I said to myself, "What the hell have I gotten into?"

After that, the kids got settled under the table and didn't make a peep down there. We talked business. I tried to remember everything Jorge told me, as I was damn sure that crazy woman wasn't paying attention, and I wrote down an address in my book for Aunt Ruth in Arizona. I forgot all about the kids until I looked down, and saw that the two of them were sitting under there picking up ants with their thumbs and pointer fingers and popping them in their mouths. Shit!

We took photos with a Polaroid, and Jorge handed them back to his cousin who had just made us the tacos, and he went into the back room, where he'd gotten the chapbook.

Jorge and I were the only ones eating. The kids stayed below with their bugs, and the mom only ordered a coke, and chain-smoked through the meal. Marcy told me about her husband, who was in prison in Mexico. I didn't really want to hear it, for obvious reasons, but she was going to tell it no matter.

"For bringing in drugs, man. Like the government doesn't take a cut. I've got to put food on the table, and I'm not turning no more tricks. That's a dead end, man. That's worse than scrubbing toilets."

I began to feel a little sorry for her. She was only twenty-four and she was already that world-weary, and then she reached down and smacked one of the kids out of nowhere, not for any reason I could surmise.

"Why'd you do that?" I asked her, sort of pissed.

"They know they're not allowed to touch my legs." Jesus, this lady was a whack job. I rolled my eyes at Jorge, and he shrugged at me. "Only white lady we could find," he said under his breath. I wanted to get away from her and her kids, not be stuck in the van with them. Those feral kids, that stoned mother: The whole thing was just so fucking depressing.

"Don't you worry you could go to jail, too?" I asked her. I wanted to ask her what her fucking problem was, but I didn't.

"Then the kids wouldn't have any parents." She shrugged. "Yeah. I think of it sometimes. And their grandparents suck, so that's no great shakes either." She wore a pendant to ward off the Evil Eye that her mother had gotten her in Turkey. It seemed that the parents had some kind of money behind them, which made the whole story all the stranger. "This has kept me safe so far. Though I don't know, man, you seem to have really negative energy."

"Me?" I laughed my ass off at this. Even Jorge was laughing. She was some kind of black witch compared to me.

Jorge stepped in. "No, no. He's a sweet guy. You're a nice lady. You two are going to get along, I promise. You're going to love each other." I gave Jorge a look, but he shook his head seriously. "You will, Mike."

Still, on the surface of it we looked good. Even the bug-eating children looked good if you sat them up and didn't let them move around too much. The cousin brought out our new papers and driver's licenses and we looked them over. Truth be told, they looked terrible. You could see the pry mark in the lamination where the cousin had wedged in the photos of our faces. It was the most half-assed fake ID I had ever seen. I imagined they used the same ones over and over, and just kept swapping out the pictures of the mules.

Jorge could see how tense I was, and he thumped me on the back.

"I promise, I promise, they are not even going to ask you for them, man. They never do."

I calmed myself down and we talked about our cover story. Didn't make up too much, as I had my worries that she wouldn't be able to remember any of it. I thought I could cover

for her somehow. She was pretty, young and white. I just looked at her and said to myself, "If I can get her to keep her mouth shut, we'll be fine."

Jorge took us to the camper, gave us the keys and registration. It was just parked on the street, stuffed to the gunnels with weed. It was a wonder you couldn't smell it three blocks away, but the guys who packed it did something right, because as far as anyone could see or smell, it was just a camper van. Not one fucking thing suspicious about it.

We hopped in. Jorge gave us each a kiss, and told me to call him from Aunt Ruth's house. We'd see each other sometime soon. He was going to be reading his poetry at a couple of places in New York City in the fall, and bye bye, that was it.

The drive to the border was uneventful, and then there was that wait for our turn to get through. So the kids were just jumping around in the back, standing on the table, even the baby, so that every time we lurched forward the kids would wobble and almost fall down and hurt themselves. I was going crazy from this. I would turn around and yell at them to get down but they acted like they couldn't even hear me.

"Marcy, get your fucking kids down! They're going to really hurt themselves!" But she hardly noticed those kids. She was just playing around with the radio and smoking cigarettes, hanging out the window, chatting with the people in the cars stopped next to ours. "Jesus Christ! Kids, get down now!"

They didn't get down. I tried to turn the car off so I could go back and get them, but just as I put it into park the cars started moving again, and the people behind me were honking. The next time we moved—just as I'd warned them—the little girl fell over and hit herself hard on the edge of the table going down. Now she started bawling. Really sobbing, and the baby, who was standing over her in her fancy playsuit, but with what was obviously a very full diaper sagging it down, started crying her ass off, too.

"Come up here," I said to her. "Let me see your arm." She was holding it and sobbing, and she got into the front seat between me and her mother, and then the other kid got in next to her, and we all were sitting up there with the kids sobbing and the mother smoking out the window and barely paying attention.

Finally I snapped.

"What the fuck is wrong with you? Your kid hurt herself and you don't even notice? What kind of a mother are you?" Marcy, who had been fiddling with her Evil Eye necklace, gave me a look, but I was just sweating it out at this point.

"Those kids just want attention. There's nothing wrong with her." That's what the bitch said then.

"Jesus Christ! Look at her fucking arm! Are you so fucking high you can't tell the difference between a broken arm and a normal one?" This got her attention, and she turned to me, and her whole spaced-out Northern California vibe totally disintegrated.

"Don't you fucking scream at me! You don't have anything to do with these fucking kids! I don't know you from Adam! You're a fucking stranger!"

And just then is when we pulled up to the border.

"Hello!" said the officer at the border, smiling at us. "Papers?" Marcy looked at him. Now she was crying, both kids were crying, and I was bright red with flecks of spittle at the corners of my mouth. We had totally forgotten where we were or where we were going, what the hell we were doing there. That the car was loaded down with prime-grade marijuana, and probably a kilo or two of cocaine that Jorge hadn't mentioned. I tried to calm myself down, but with the whole front seat filled with crying females, I could hardly do it.

"Look," I said to the officer, "the older one just fell off the table at the back. I think she broke her arm." My hand was shaking. "I forgot to get out the papers. I'm not even sure where we put them." That was the truth. Can you believe it? I didn't even know where those fake papers were.

The officer took one look at the girls, at Marcy, and at my face, and he said, "Hey, I hear you. It's one of those days. Go get that kid to the doctor." And then he waved us on through the gate, with a metric shit-ton of grass in the walls of that fucking camper van.

As for the kids, that woman, and the rest of it, we took the kid to the hospital to get her arm checked out, and it was broken, after all. Of course it was broken. Only a drooling idiot couldn't see that, which that fucking Marcy was. Aunt Ruth came to pick up the van from there, and he and I called Jorge from a payphone in the lobby. I called in an old girlfriend to come and talk to that bitch, and see if she could get her to send her kids back to her mother or something, anything else but that piece of shit Marcy looking out for them, and my ex-girlfriend has such a sweet touch that she got her to agree.

That year I didn't work once. I wrote a book, and treated my friends to steak dinners. It was fast money, but I wouldn't exactly call it easy. Still, it wasn't a job that a couple of Morenos could have pulled off, if you get my drift. ❧

1

Lickey Louse & his public defender
in

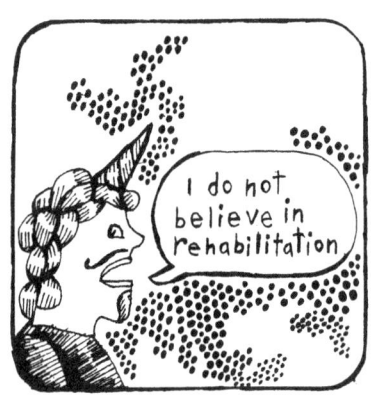

Colloquium At the End of the World

On empowerment, critical thinking, and the purpose of education in the last days of the American experiment

A used-book review by
Anicula

ALL CHAOS and deterioration in present society come from a raging and apparent crisis in American education, one that we have failed to address successfully or to remediate for several generations. Coast to coast we are turning out kids—people—who are functionally literate in the sense of phonemes alone. They can in no way sift through the piles of rhetorical obfuscation and inanity or make sense of the complications of a world made overly complicated by the sales force of capitalism. Because of this, the crooks and con men have come out ahead, exploiting the vulnerabilities of an undereducated populace and leading us to our present situation. Yet we can't blame them for following their natural inclinations, nor can we demand a perfect world because we are not up to the task of self-defense. Or rather, we can, but that is no kind of a tactic.

Without the tools to find the true sources of our discomfort, the American trade is now in conspiracy theory, panicked distrust, and an overall sense of dis-ease that colors our everyday lives. We have made these fears manifest in our current administration, but they were there long before. We neither trust nor understand the mechanics of our democracy; there is even some talk, among Americans, in appreciation of monarchies.[1] All, from the left to the right, worship celebrities, wealth and moral bankruptcy, or at least all who are audible do so. Just as many people have lost the taste for non-flavor-blasted food, we've all lost our taste for subtler truths, nuance and measured ideas that take into consideration more than one perspective; our palates are not primed for them, so we can't taste them at all. And, yes, I'm laying this all at the feet of the American system of education.

Obviously this is too much for us to address, and certainly too much for that poor and disenfranchised group who hobble around the country with their wheelie carts full of ungraded papers, patching up their broken-down Hyundais with Elmer's School Glue, and gripping their pre-ulcerous stomach conditions, like the most unhappy and unsuccessful of Napoleons. I'm referring, of course, to our nation's educators. Who can blame anyone for sitting it out? We busy ourselves overeating, smoking weed, and watching television; anything else feels beyond our abilities and our pay grade. After all, catastro-

---

[1] Leslie Wayne, "The World Could Use More Kings and Queens, Monarchists Say," *New York Times*, January 6, 2018.

phe assails us on all sides. To which direction should we turn first? Let us, like Hobbits, till our gardens and smoke our pipes until the bitter end, when the whole world falls into a warm and churning sea. Okay?[2]

It takes some degree of brain damage—no long-term memory, perhaps, or no sense of futurity—or more reasonably a core of resilient religious or ethical principles to stay in this particular fight, the fight for the whole culture.

This book was written because we are serious, dedicated, professional educators, which means that we are simple, romantic men who risk contributing to the mental-health problem by maintaining a belief in the improvability of the human condition through education.[3]

It is romantics alone who will wade into this one. So say the authors of *Teaching as a Subversive Activity* in their introduction to the book. These are the two hippie bastards—nés college professors—Neil Postman and Charles Weingartner, who present us with this tract and informal workbook, though pictures of Postman do not show him to be a long-hair at all. He looks like a rather clean-cut educator, though maybe his hair is a little long. (As for Weingartner, the Internet has lost him, and it's much too cold this winter to go out to Queen's College just for a picture.) Hippie bastards, I say, then, because the book from cover to last page projects their countercultural purpose.

After all, the cover of my edition, and most others, is a picture of a weaponized apple, fuse lit. And where are they planning on throwing it? Not as con-

---

[2] And perhaps we would actually do that if teachers had money for the down payment on the house with the garden, but since we don't, I suppose we will all have to be radicals.

[3] Neil Postman and Charles Weingartner, *Teaching As a Subversive Activity* (New York: Delta, 1969), p. xiii.

[4] The address, called "Bullshit and the Art of Crap-Detecting," was delivered to the National Council of Teachers of English in 1969. That year the organization took a stance against the Vietnam War, and in other ways addressed the multiplicity of political crises in American society, so Postman's address, though extreme, was not out of step. "In 1969 . . . we bused to DC for a quite different NCTE Convention, a 'Dreams and Realities' theme, where James Moffett's address, 'Coming on Center,' would rock many of us—the first time, I suspect, I heard a teacher-leader use the phrase military industrial complex! . . . Ultimately, those assembled passed a resolution in which 'the Council officially expresses its abhorrence of the Viet Nam War and its desire to see this divisive conflict ended.' . . . Alex Haley . . . told the story of his research, of looking for ancestors in property records, and of his journey to Africa, from which he had just returned, to successfully locate his

Something is wrong with the world as it is, and school, as a reflection of that world, is a profoundly alienating and toxic place.

frontational as Neil Postman's address to the NCTE conference that same year.[4] But confrontational. Herein we will learn what is wrong with us and our systems, be excoriated for our straight ways, and asked to pick a side (or rather be hectored into picking their side, since no one who picked up the book, especially in 1969, would choose the side that is out of touch with the kids and, frankly, out of style). In general, we will get a nice ice bath of a reality check about our egos and our priorities. Think of it as a New Year's Day Polar Bear swim for educational Heads. Though this is not how modern people might take it, it certainly was intended that way. Today, as always, is never a bad time to "get right with God," and, as we knew by 1969, it only takes five seconds to do so. We all need to dunk our heads sometimes—look over our own motives, find out if they are pure, or if we are guided by bullshit and our egos—if we are going to contribute to progress. And progress is our issue here, progress our national problem. The mule of state has stubbornly mired itself in mud, and we, as teachers, have got to figure out where best to deliver the kick. As a sign at the 2018 Women's March put it: "We haven't come this far, to only come this far."

The authors of *Teaching as a Subversive Activity* hold us accountable for the systems to which we contribute, and believe that good educators need to look at them, and ourselves, critically. Here is a manual for practitioners, and if you are not a practitioner, there is still much you can get out of this.

Something is wrong with the world as it is, and school, as a reflection of that world, is a profoundly alienating and toxic place. They are talking of their own contemporaneous world; students in 1969 were alienated, bored, angry, and destined to drop out. However, in 2018, the students feel pretty close to the same. The 2018

family and tribe. A silent, awestruck audience followed his tracing through oral history of a few syllables in a native language and at the end gave the most spontaneous and sustained standing ovation of which I have ever been a part. . . . I have not thought of NCTE as apolitical since 1969." From "What Challenges Might We Embrace, and How?" by James Davis, quoting NCTE member Doug Hesse in a post to the Teaching and Learning Forum, November 12, 2016.

students, however, know that no one gives a shit if they drop out or do any other harm to themselves. The world's utter indifference to them, their plight, and that of their families is patent, especially for the poor—as it has ever been—but now even for middle class families. In the sixties the threats and recriminations of the kids impacted the culture—in many ways the culture changed for them—but now the culture has learned, and can shrug off almost anything.

'I think a lot of the trouble comes from a lack of love between students and teachers,' 19-year-old George McLauglin added.

All political activity, like union activity, requires, on some level, an antagonist with a stake in the same system. Not a stake in the well-being of the opposing side, but in the existence of an ecosystem which includes both sides. But if your antagonist is a pure nihilist? Why bother bargaining if, with no compunction at all, you can simply move the work elsewhere, or take down the whole company? (See the case of the web site Gothamist,[5] which was shut down almost immediately after the contributors voted to unionize.) When those in charge don't care at all about you—when there are, for instance, businessmen, not educators, in charge of education—what could be less relevant than a student's plea for humanity? The students today know better.

But if we were to care, how would we go about it? How would we reconnect the students with their institutions, assuming that reconnecting them with their institutions is the way to reconnect them with their democracy, from which they, like all of us, are clearly alienated?

The book advocates for an inquiry method, rather than the top-down pedagogy of a lecturer, an "expert." The students' questions form the curriculum, subjects fuse, and teachers drop the didactic transmission of material for something student-driven. All fair, though the modern reader, who has gone looking for insight and a new workable premise, is a trifle pained. I suppose that's what one gets when one looks for futurity in a long-ago world. What was radical in 1969 is old news now. Group work, multidisciplinary education, learning by doing. The misuse of these old

---

[5] Andy Newman and John Leland, "DNAinfo and Gothamist Are Shut Down After Votes to Unionize," *New York Times*, November 2, 2017.

workhorse ideas has led directly to that Frankensteinian system we have now, where the students don't care, have no personal investment, *and* don't know any grammar.

Further ideas unfold, of quiet purity. They are also in no way radical, but are still important to hear. Do not hate your students. Question your own behavior and intentionality. Are you conveying a lack of confidence in your students' abilities? "If teachers acted as if their students were meaning makers, almost everything about the school process would change."[6]

The authors, taking us future people with them into the alien land of the late sixties, quote from an article describing a scene in a high school auditorium. A panel of teenagers has been convened, the sort of panel frequently convened in the 1960s and 70s. The teachers, somewhat understandably, become thorny, though the authors—who clearly have not been on the receiving end of a long list of true but unnecessarily stated recriminations from their spouses, or at least did not extrapolate anything from that experience—have no sympathy for that: "We think it safe to assume that the teachers who left because they couldn't 'take it any longer' are useless in the new education."[7] These panels are scenes out of any revolution, though this one doesn't end with the bosses tied up, or swabbing out the toilets, as it might have in the Cultural Revolution or in the Godard version.[8] But the students' plea is basic, and even a little poignant:

"I think a lot of the trouble comes from a lack of love between students and teachers," 19-year-old *George McLauglin added.*

"It's not my job to love my pupils—it's my job to teach them," a teacher shouted back.[9]

To my disrelish, I can imagine any number of specific teachers I have known over the years shouting back such a thing, or at least muttering it audibly.

---

[6] Postman, p. 92.

[7] Ibid., p. 136.

[8] See *Tout Va Bien*. A factory is taken over. Fat cats—and Jane Fonda, incongruously— are held hostage. See too *Blood in the Water*, the recent book on the Attica revolt. See too the contemporaneous story of the teachers held hostage in their auditorium. (Though I can't find any mention of it, and am starting to wonder whether it was an old wives' tale, passed on by enraged teachers to their grandchildren.) Whatever were their outcomes, panels, people tied up, and public recriminations were the revolutionary tactics in those days.

[9] Postman, p. 135.

The idea that a teacher thinks he will have luck transmitting information to a population that he clearly despises and looks down on is not such an old or an outdated idea. These sentiments are clear in any public system, are clear all up and down the line, but especially so in lower-level colleges, where the professors have gone to great lengths to distinguish themselves with their PhDs and publications. To them, the students' low levels seem to reflect on their own personal failings. These feelings are only partially concealed by the teachers in question, and come out in any number of verbal tics and private conversations.

The authors have taken it upon themselves to state what sane people might consider an obvious point, that it is impossible to teach effectively kids you actively dislike: "Bear in mind that it is probably not possible for such [inquiry-based] learning to occur unless there is something resembling a loving relationship between 'teacher' and learner."[10] Not just a relationship of bland toleration, but an actual loving relationship. How many times in your own schooling has the cruelty of a teacher, their sharp voice alone, or their cutting sense of humor, shut down your memory and capacity for learning? (Or maybe you are the son of a traditional Jewish household who thrived under that sort of teaching, and are now a grandmaster, or Rahm Emmanuel? Certainly, we should leave the world to you resilient souls!)

For all the book's simple truths and tired-out tropes and plans, there is a radical idea contained within: A teacher should try to be a present human being in the classroom; not simply an "expert," but a mortal being with cares, opinions, sorrows, loves and fears. To be themselves with their students, people who are, as Ram Dass says, "walking each other home":

And the teacher became aware of a special dimension in education that, on a large scale, has never been explored or studied: what the teacher has to say of a personal and compelling nature to students.[11]

That the teacher has something to say of a "personal and compelling nature to students" is, to this day, an unheard-of idea. In fact, most practical advice offered up to new teachers implies that you should never bring your real self into the

---

[10]Ibid., p. 140.
[11]Ibid., p. 174.

classroom: "Don't smile for the first month," "Don't tell them your first name, lest they use it," etc. Some of this is the advice of self-preservation in rough classrooms, especially laid out for new teachers who wear their victimhood on their soft and puzzled brows. All of us have heard the myriad stories of teachers murdered after interacting with students outside of school.[12] But these stories are red herrings, and clearly no one sane recommends giving out your home telephone number, or having anyone over. Being present while in the classroom is the idea here.

If you are a teacher, when was the last time you wrote something to a pupil so that he could comment on your idea? . . . But perhaps teachers have nothing to communicate to students. Perhaps they are afraid to talk with them. Maybe that's what lesson plans are all about— a tactical diversion so that no one need say anything to anyone.[13]

Of course, being revolutionaries,

It is impossible to teach effectively kids you actively dislike.

there is a hectoring tinge to their tone. Why should anyone feel ashamed of making lesson plans? And what exactly is the difference between the pre-planning that the authors suggest—and they do suggest work outside the classroom—and what another type of teacher might write down more formally? Is it the idea of a plan on paper that leads to hegemony? It is reductive of them, but my mention of it is a quibble. There is a revolutionary idea, an idea that feels new to me even now, in all its ramifications.

The authors advocate for a question-based approach to learning, and even have the courtesy to leave us our own blank page for the purpose of writing questions in the chapter entitled "What's Worth Knowing." (Though they do spend a great deal of time immediately after implying that our choice of questions was a bit off. And as jazzed as I felt to write down my questions— with which I filled the whole page—I felt chastened immediately after.)[14] In response to their

---

[12]Matthew Purdy, "Manhunt Leads to Two Arrests in Levin Killing," *New York Times*, June 8, 1997.

[13]Postman, pp. 174–175.

[14]Ibid., p. 65: "The new education is a process and *will not suffer* [emphasis mine, as opposed to *will benefit*] from the applied imaginations of all who wish to be a part of it. But in evaluating your own questions, as well as ours, bear in mind that here are certain standards that must be used." Best to make the rules and standards evident before you ask the student to do the work, not after, teachers!

An effective teacher must not require his ego to be petted, his mood to be lifted, or even that his students connect with him.

suggestion of bringing our authentic self into the classroom, I will now begin with a question: What can a teacher get out of this type of classroom that makes the work worth his or her time?

If you are an educator, especially an administrator, this may seem to you like a crazy question, and certainly it is the kind of question, to put it mildly, that teachers are not encouraged to ask. After all, you don't ask a dentist what he gets out of it beyond money and professional pride. But the teacher does not get money, and every step along the way he is thwarted from having professional pride. Therefore we must be talking about something beyond that.

The transition to a "new" style of classroom asks for something more from the teacher, a real investment and engagement that is different from what most other people bring to their jobs, more along the lines of the engagement most people bring to their families. If there is no real engagement— actual buy-in—being asked to bring in your authentic self seems coercive, like the enthusiasm for the act shown by a paid sex worker, or the emotional connection that a manicurist evinces who has to chat up clients she despises.

Such lying about the needs of the self is patriarchal women's work, and consequently something New People cannot retain as a job requirement. So let's transgress entirely for a moment, forget about the student, and ask: "What's in it for the teacher?"

The system would have to change all the way for this coercive aspect of Inquiry-Based Education to change. Having gone through a master's degree program in education, and all those Saturday morning professional development classes one is required to take for teaching certification, I know intimately how little any person, either teacher or student, wants to be forced to perform their "true soul" for an audience. This is doubly so when the teacher is profoundly stupid, and one was forced to take the class in the first place. The authors make it clear at several points in the book that their ideas work best in electives, but unless we plan to change the laws, school itself, like teacher licensing requirements, is not an elective. Have sympathy for those students, young and old, who want to come to class and do a worksheet some mornings without coercion, or who would rather not talk about their lives and opinions with a particular teacher for their own very good reasons.

I am aware that the examples of painful education classes primarily show teachers teaching poorly, but it doesn't really matter. It's hard to be in classes that ask for authenticity day in and day out, but give little in return, much harder than attending poor but workaday classes, where at least if you apply yourself, you will learn some skills by the end of them. Uninspired people pretending to be inspired is an ugly thing, and how many genuinely inspired and alive people do you meet in your lifetime? Enough to populate the entire faculty of one large public high school? I haven't. I felt this even while reading *Teaching as a Subversive Activity*, as I did so often when I was reading education texts in school.

Sometimes the tone of revolutionary ferment, or enthusiasm, feels misplaced, and maybe your revolutionary ferment is my ho-hum—even were it not the ferment of fifty years ago; the starter must clearly be dead already—and I shouldn't have to pretend to sign on for the sake of your ego. (The taming of ego, all teachers of this sort agree, being the basis of reasonable teaching. But more on that later.) How different is the revolutionary tone of expertise from that other tone of expertise that the authors excoriate? Where is the tentative quietude which, say the authors themselves, is vital to modeling real investigation? Despite what they say, they sound just as didactic as the much-loathed podium lecturers they continually rebuke.[15] Neither do they cop to the idea that all they are describing is experimental; their certitude has not been validated by subsequent history.

Ego in the classroom is addressed by the following requirement: that each teacher have at least one person in the world who will attest to their love for that person.[16] An effective teacher must

---

[15] Two examples out of the many instances of recrimination against this attitude and behavior: Ibid., p. 19: "Now what is it that students do in the classroom? Well, mostly, they sit and listen to the teacher. Mostly, they are required to believe in authorities, or at least pretend to such belief to take tests." And p. 42: "There are thousands of teachers who teach . . . because they are inclined to talk about such matters. In fact, that is why they became teachers. It is also why their students fail to become competent learners. There are thousands of teachers who define a 'bad' student as any student who doesn't respond to what has been prescribed for him."

[16] Ibid., p. 140: "Require each teacher to provide some sort of evidence that he or she has had a loving relationship with at least one other human being. If the teacher can get someone to say, 'I love her (or him),' she should be retained. If she can get two people to say it, she should get a raise. Spouses need not be excluded from testifying."

not require his ego to be petted, his mood to be lifted, or even that his students connect with him. Why should that be a requirement for school? They may not like you. You may not like them. Just as a matter of personal chemistry. You must have someone else, who has chosen you, to care about you.

Of course, I get a vague wave of pity and sorrow when I think of all those public school teachers whom I've known over the years who were obviously and utterly without joy, love, or any positive emotion in any part of their lives. What should be done for them? During four years at a large public high school, one heavy-drinking young woman died of a stroke, orphaning her two little girls, and a woman in the business department jumped out of her apartment window. That might not seem like a high percentage—though imagine if you worked at a tech start-up and this was the same percentage in your office in the same amount of time—but at the time it did, and certainly it felt more than coincidental to the surroundings. I've heard of one suicide at my new position. I certainly have seen and talked to some very sad people over the years.

It is the schools to blame for the unhappiness of their teachers, though mental illness and poor health are the literal reasons. And those who are "unloved and unlovable," as the book might put it, were perhaps made that way by the institutions in which they teach. The teachers' lives at these places are much too difficult, and the stress they feel ratchets up all year and never abates. Whether the administration demands test scores or eye contact, it is the fact of an administration-that-demands which makes the job impossible.

Yet the authors might be right, that unloved teachers are part of the problem. The great misery and unhappiness of the teachers creates a feedback loop that makes the students unhappy, too. That has not changed between 1969 and now. (Unless we believe that the students are also part of the problem, which we do. The behavior that the students bring to the classroom reflects on their own mental conditions, as well. It is part of the backdrop of misery that decorates many inner-city schools.)

Many people believe that the love and good cheer of the teachers is irrelevant anyway. Many believe that the more challenged the students are, the more doctrinaire should be their teachers. *The New Yorker* recently published a most painful exposé of the Success Academies, places where little children sit and talk like robots, tracking teachers with their eyes, disallowed *It is the fact of an administration-that-demands which makes the job impossible.* from moving in their tiny drawn boxes on the rugs, marched silently in the halls from room to room, and dropped quickly from the school for minor infractions.[17] The author's tone made it clear what she thought— the piece was a hatchet job—and despite the popularity of these schools, they ought to be a hard sell for real educators who have read the literature. Said a letter sent in response:

Schools that are focussed on "achievement" (which is measured mostly by test scores) and on "discipline" (which usually restricts choice and movement) tend to serve poor children of color in large cities. In wealthier neighborhoods, progressive education in the tradition of John Dewey and Deborah Meier is the norm. Many of us in education have long seen the movement towards stricter schools for what it is: an approach steeped in racism.[18]

Yet the issue here, and the discussion topic, is not the schools to which rich kids go. Those schools are now, and have always been, fine, one way or another. This discussion is, as most discussions end up being nowadays, a discussion of class. Because we as a society do not invest in our public education, this broken system is what we get, and I don't mean just the broken system of public education, but the broken system of our government. Teachers on the ground, especially those paid poverty wages with no expectation at all of professional respect, fall back on these joyless methods.

---

[17] Rebecca Mead, "Success Academy's Radical Educational Experiment," *New Yorker*, December 11, 2017. "In the second-grade classroom in Queens, the gridded rug seemed less like a magic carpet than like a chessboard at the start of a game. Within each square was a large colored spot the size of a chair cushion. The children sat in rows, facing forward, each within his or her assigned square, with their legs crossed and their hands clasped or folded in their laps. Success students can expect to be called to answer a teacher's question at any moment, not just when they raise their hand, and must keep their eyes trained on the speaker at all times, a practice known as 'tracking.' Staring off into space, or avoiding eye contact, is not acceptable. 'Sometimes when kids look like they're daydreaming, it's because they are, and we can't allow that possibility,' Moskowitz wrote a few years ago, in an editorial for the *Wall Street Journal*. Students who stop tracking are prodded both by their teachers and by their peers, who are expected to point out classmates who aren't looking at them when they are speaking."

[18] Pax Linson, letter to the editor, *New Yorker*, January 8, 2018.

Neil Postman

Since I myself most enjoy reading the case studies and real-life examples in educational texts, I will offer one of my own. Recently, the following conversation ensued in my school's adjunct-teachers' lounge. This is a place, like all teachers' lounges at public institutions, that moves rapidly between hilarity and the final push off the ledge, depending on your mood on a given day (a fifteen-minute considered discussion of what is on offer in the cafeteria—the tastes and aesthetics—when the

food before them is sad boiled chicken and ziti on a styrofoam plate; an argument about Miranda laws between the Ignoramus and the Paranoiac, who end up in a stand-off, maneuvering around printers and file cabinets, neither remotely accurate as to facts; harsh recriminations of colleagues guilty of minute transgressions around printers and file cabinets; and so on).

With the knowledge that I am unfairly categorizing these undeserving souls, who are God's creatures, and themselves deserving of love and respect, whether or not they are profound jackasses, I present to you the following scene: We are in the adjunct-teachers' lounge with a somewhat overeager older WOMAN who is interested in approval from a younger MAN who is himself somewhat past his prime but still looking like he has places to be (a white man, of course, with nice hair).

W: Your class was incredible! That's the best writing I've ever seen!

M: Thanks. Yeah, they are a good class. (He takes the superlative in stride.)

W: How do you do it? How is their writing so incredible?

M (with confidence, yet dismissive of the older woman, and, most sympathetically, desirous to get out of the conversation): I use templates. They're very effective.

W: Amazing! They really are! Can I get a copy? (Man clearly doesn't want to, but agrees, out of forced politeness, to share the templates.)

A WOMAN ACROSS THE ROOM pipes up.

WATR: I'd like a copy, too. (Man sighs, but agrees to give her a copy, too.)

(CURTAIN)

More information is needed here to fully understand this scene. I would be unfairly stacking the deck for my argument if I didn't acknowledge that the classes being discussed were remedial, and the students in them needed very badly to pass a test in order to remain in college. So perhaps what they really needed was a template. That's probably true, but it's a massive bummer that anyone would call the work reaped from the template "the best writing I have ever seen" without adding the qualifier "from these challenged students." To be fair, this must have been what she meant, though she did not say it.

Are there times in life when students should be given templates for their writing? About that I'm not certain. Though, when preparing super-seniors who had failed the Regents multiple times, I've certainly come as close as I'm ever going to get.

And, quite frankly, should students who need templates be enrolled in colleges, junior or otherwise? What is college, then? Am I, myself, missing some basic understanding of the purpose of community college, due to a snobbery about higher education? Does their presence there undermine the hard work of all the kids from similar backgrounds who can write well enough to pass the test? Or is this actually and only a problem of how to integrate newer arrivals into our beloved and ecumenical Nation of Immigrants?

All valid questions for which I have no answers.

Across the continuum from templates, it turns out that I am also wary of an overabundance of progressivism. I am wary of any discussion of education that concerns itself with revolutionary methods, though I am in favor of revolutionary content, or, since the medium is the message and I can't reasonably make the distinction, I am in favor of the content of revolution, and will sometimes have to put up with the means of its transmission.

I went to education school at a time when Gardner and his multiple intelligences,[19] was taken so for granted that the ideas in E. D. Hirsch's book *Cultural Literacy*[20] (that a traditional canon was necessary for society and for the students; that their education should not be touchy-feely, but rigorous and curriculum-based) were already back and gaining ascendancy. And now, it seems, with the emphasis on rules and tests that I hear about from all sides, we are back where we started. The pendulum has swung over the crowd several times since my own graduate education. This present swing is in direct response to the experimental inquiry-based ideas that had taken hold for the last few generations. Many of the books I read at the time discussed the use of inquiry-based methods in inner-city classrooms. It is interesting to note that many of the authors of such books got out of the classroom after only a year or two,[21] well before they would have gotten to the point of mastery, which, common knowledge says, whether you are adopting a conventional or a subversive approach, occurs in the third year of teaching.[22]

Assuredly, teachers flame out more quickly when they are teaching in a creative, inquiry style. It is much more work to invent the world anew every year according to your particular students, than to fill in a year's worth of schooldays with worksheets and quizzes that can be printed out the same

---

[19] Howard Gardner, *Frames of Mind: The Theory of Multiple Intelligences* (Basic Books, 1983).

[20] E. D. Hirsch, *Cultural Literacy: What Every American Needs to Know* (Knopf Doubleday, 1988).

[21] According to his Wikipedia page, Jonathan Kozol, author of *Death at an Early Age*, "taught [in Newton, MA] for several years before becoming more deeply involved in social justice work and dedicating more time to writing." After four years, Erin Gruwell, author of Freedom Writers, later to be an inspirational pic staring Hillary Swank, went on to start a foundation and become a motivational speaker.

[22] However, if you should be curious, as with all human experiences, it only takes one year of teaching to get a book out of it!

way year after year. You must only change the date atop the page. A teacher who is truly invested and engaged to the maximum degree puts in ridiculous hours in addition to the time in school, and when you factor in the bad pay and the rest of it, I would argue that only the most anointed can keep that up beyond a year or two.

This brings me back to that key question: The authors tell us that a truly free educational system requires teachers who love the students, who have experienced something of life,[23] who enjoy their work, and who don't want to bug out after one year, when they still don't know the ropes. (I add this: The authors don't mention the high rates of turnover, perhaps not having seen them yet.) So how do you create a system that is egosyntonic for the teacher? What does the teacher get out of it, because if they don't get something out of it, they're not going to stay. Unless, of course, like charter schools, we want a Holly-

Assuredly, teachers flame out more quickly when they are teaching in a creative, inquiry style.

wood machine of nubile teaching starlets, those that are particularly malleable, and have no boundaries that might prevent them from going along with unreasonable demands.

Anti-unionists and charter school aficionados always say that we hear too much already about the needs of the teachers, but that's clearly ridiculous—propaganda that works only on fools and martyrs, and which takes advantage of the weaknesses of a majority-female workforce who have been brought up in a patriarchy and are easily shamed by being told that they are selfish. There is no conflict between the needs of the students and the needs of the teachers. Whatever serves the teachers and makes them comfortable (this is of course assuming you are hiring teachers and not some other sort of humans) serves the students in the end. If a teacher needs her coffee on the desk or to sit down or to have a bathroom break, she remains a person in a body that must be kept calm and stable in

---

[23] Postman, pp. 139–140: "Require every teacher to take a one-year leave of absence every fourth year to work in some 'field' other than education. Such an experience can be taken as evidence, albeit shaky, that the teacher has been in contact with reality at some point in his life. Recommended occupations: bartender, cab driver, garment worker, waiter. One of the common sources of difficulty with teachers can be found in the fact that most of them simply move from one side of the desk (as students) to the other (as 'teachers') and they have not had much contact with the way things are outside of school rooms."

order to function. A mother with the flu can't do a great job with her kids. A surgeon with a broken hand can't operate, and a teacher with situational depression and alcoholism from being REMFed and otherwise undermined by administration,[24] from their work conditions, from screaming and troubled students who aren't getting the support they need, and from public disopprobrium, can't bring love and light to their students. At best what they can do is reflect back the pain and difficulty the students themselves are feeling. That's not nothing when it comes to forming a connection, but neither does it communicate a way out, or model professional pride for the students.

A subversive classroom must be geared to the needs of the teacher. She must both captain it, and find comfort there. It must be a place that conforms to her opinions, dreams, and desires, even as it is that for the students, as well. Which is to say, right now with things as they are in public schools, there is almost nothing in it for the teachers.

All of this is why Postman and

> *A decent teacher must be a revolutionary, for the world, and the schools, meet neither her, nor her students', needs.*

Weingartner are right in their conclusions. When taking account of the educational system as it is, the world as it is, a decent teacher must be a revolutionary, for the world, and the schools, meet neither her, nor her students', needs. She must teach revolution, foment revolution, and make revolution the subject of the classroom. If we learn by doing, as the authors and pretty much everyone else since then suggests, then the fact of our confinement ("our" meaning that of the teacher and the student both, for the awareness of the mutuality of our confinement is key to the revolutionary classroom) ought to be the first premise of our modern curriculum. The medium does, in fact, remain the message. What we do together within this confinement, how we take stock of the physicality of the walls and bars on the windows, is the work we do together. (This doesn't work if the teacher is a highly paid and respected professional. They must find their own way. This approach is appropriate for adjuncts, inner-city public school teachers, and anyone for whom the terms of their em-

---

[24]REMF stands for Rear Echelon Motherfucker. Slang from the Vietnam War that means the asshole who hangs out behind you backseat-driving.

ployment is contingent on their financial vulnerability, lack of self-respect, and lack of other options.)

To teach the reality of confinement, one must practice transparency. This was a stock term when I came up in the system, but what was meant by it was some sort of metacognitive scaffolding, the idea that you showed the students what you were trying to teach them at all times. What is meant by transparency here is an honest display of your own feelings about the parts of the system, rules, etc., that don't jibe with your own beliefs. When it's bullshit, call it out. This implies that you yourself know and feel when it's bullshit. The authors see this as a central aspect of their approach, and began the book with the topic of so-called crap-detecting. As Hemingway said—it is his term—"in order to be a great writer a person must have a built-in, shockproof crap detector." "It seems," the writers go on, that "Hemingway identified an essential survival strategy and the essential function of the schools in today's world."[25] This is clearly what is missing in society at large. All of our bullshit detectors, Left and Right, are on the fritz. Or, should we be more elegant individuals (atavists, at this point), our critical thinking skills are almost entirely absent.

A crap detector sees and analyzes the crap around him. As the authors tell us: "It is the sign of a competent 'crap detector' that he is not completely captivated by the arbitrary abstractions of the community in which he happened to grow up."[26] Or as Postman says in his confrontational NCTE speech from 1969: "Every day in almost every way people are exposed to more bullshit than is healthy for them to endure," and, the authors imply, it is the job of the teachers to help them not to be acted upon by this bullshit that they are forced to endure. The answers to our cultural failings are right here. But what is meant by it? And surely, you are mildly put out: "I, as a Leftist, cannot be placed in the same category as those loons on the Right!" Fair enough. Yet—and it can be a family secret for just our enormous and varied, though Leftist, tribe—we too traffic in bullshit all up and down the line. Oversimplification and deifying celebrities, misery poker and senseless snobberies based on erudite and hermetic tastes. All of that, I assure you, is a modern Leftist brand of bullshit.

Most ironically, schools, today

[25] Postman, p. 3.
[26] Ibid., p. 5.

and then, are the nexus of bull-shit. This is especially ironic in high schools, since teenagers are the most alert to and horrified by signs of bullshit. But teachers, no different than other adults, are frequently steeped in it. Most adults need some kind of bullshit in order to live. A man with a truly gimlet eye could not make it through a day of what we've got here.

Q: But if I call out the bullshit to my classes—if I draw their attention to all bullshit everywhere—how can I get my students to do the bullshit required by my administration and the state?

A: It is much easier to get students to do bullshit if they know you think it's bullshit than if they think you yourself, their guide in the system, are full of shit. The amount that students and teachers can see themselves as allied against the system is the strength of their solidarity. I.e., if you want teaching and learning to get done, you better strive for some unified state along those lines. I.e., you all need to be pulling in the same direction.

Q: If you believe in a revolutionary classroom, how can you waste your time, and theirs, giving the students bullshit to do?

A: Students can't drop out and expect to thrive. Most teachers need their jobs. They can't do the

educational equivalent of a hunger strike each time some new bullshit comes up. This is why the authors' choice of the word subversion is a more appropriate and apt term than revolution, though the term revolution feels more pleasing, because it is above-board. All the same, as a teacher I've never had to put up with the levels of bullshit with which those fourth grade teachers have, forced to spend the whole year preparing for the test, prodding weeping children with an academic stick. So I'm being glib. Perhaps if I had, I'd have no truck with subversion and be heading right towards total revolt.

But after we've called out the crap, what are we left with? The authors advocate transparency in our answers to this, too:

Good learners do not need to have an absolute, final, irrevocable resolution to every problem. The sentence, "I don't know," does not depress them, and they certainly prefer it to the various forms of semantic nonsense that pass for "answers" to questions that do not as yet have any solution—or may never have one.[27]

Quite frankly, I have no idea. I suspect now we're back once again to building a civil society, a project

---

[27]Ibid., pp. 32–33.

A good teacher works to clear up the basic truths that have been hidden on purpose.

with which we've only had sporadic luck. I do know from my own ex- perience that if you consistently call out bullshit (and know accurately what bullshit looks like) then your students will see that, at the very least, you mean what you say. Which is to say, you will have created an authentic classroom in at least this one way. Which is the first step to making a place where both your students and you want to be every day.

Whatever I can say about the content of this book—and I believe I've said enough; by now I'm thor- oughly winded—mostly I've been keeping this paperback (or rather the two copies of this paperback that I have, one from each of my parents) around for years because I like to look at the title on my way to work. *Teaching as a Subver- sive Activity* as opposed to Teach- ing as a Slog, Teaching as a Day Job, Teaching as an Exercise in your Own Pedantry, Teaching as Another Option.

A subversive teacher is no dif- ferent from a political organizer, if the organizer has set their sights on evanescent goals, rather than getting a union started at a plant. The buy-in this organizer asks for is to life, truth, and the good fight

that is the move to- ward progress and freedom for all. The primary interaction a subversive teacher has with her students is akin to the interaction between Norma Rae and the organizer Reuben Warshowsky. Norma Rae asks him, "How did you get so smart?" To which Warshowsky replies: "Books." To be reductive—and why not reduce it a little, like a good thick sauce cooked down from its disparate parts—this is the central interaction of a functional class- room. Like a good organizer, a good teacher works to clear up the basic truths that have been kept hidden on purpose; demystifies the process of liberation which is of course what education is; works to make themselves obsolete; and then leaves town. That last, in the end—requiring nothing in re- turn from your students—is the ul- timate subversion.

So what are we doing here, and what is the final goal of this subver- sive classroom? With a clear eye and mind, hopefully, our students will rise above the cultural prison in which we all find ourselves.

Q: How do you plot your es- cape?

A: Know the plans of the place. ❧

Fruit Quasis

For 5-Fold Flavor!

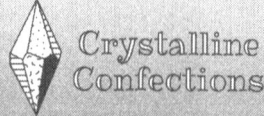

Crystalline
Confections

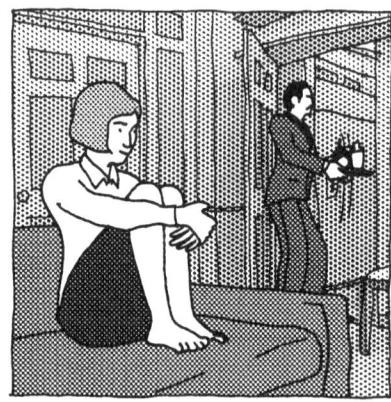

YOU'RE NOT **SAD** ABOUT SOMETHING, ARE YOU?

NO...

BUT YOU JUST ABOUT BROKE MY HEART.

WHERE DOES THAT COME FROM?

BEFORE WE MET I HAD OTHER GIRLFRIENDS.

YOU KNOW THAT, RIGHT?

YES.

AND EVERY ONE OF THOSE RELATIONSHIPS ENDED IN HEARTBREAK, DIDN'T IT?

AS FAR AS I KNOW.

MY REPERTOIRE IS NOT TOTALLY MY OWN.

THAT'S TRUE.

YOUR SUBSCRIBERS DO SHOW UP WITH ... EXPECTATIONS.

IT MAY NOT BE TRUE OF ALL LATIN MEN, BUT I THINK YOU WILL AGREE THAT I AM A STEREOTYPICALLY GREAT LOVER.

RATTLE! RATTLE! RATTLE!

IT WOULD BE FOOLISH OF ME TO DENY IT, HUSBAND.

PLUS IT'S GOOD FOR YOUR BOTTOM LINE.

I'LL DRINK TO THAT!

NEXT: "I DO REMEMBER"

find-your-center[fold]

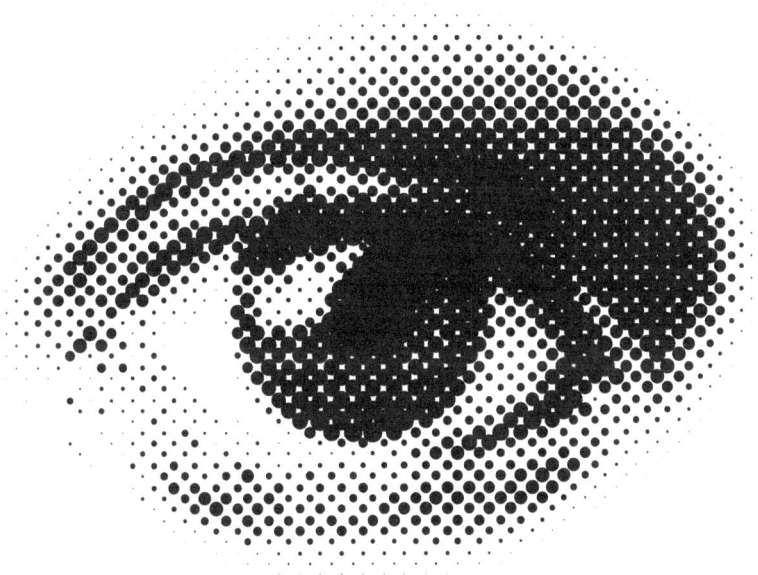

ON the following spread you will see an ornate pattern designed as a peaceful lacuna in the difficulty of your day.

Use this page as a meditation aid to slow your breath, to open your heart, and to let your third eye wink to consciousness.

Sit comfortably in your seat, or on the floor if you like, and take a deep breath in through your nose and out through your mouth. Repeat this action several times, slowing down your breathing as you go.

Then turn the page and let your eyes wander over the page. Take equal time with the spots on the page where there is no ink. Let your eyes fall into them.

Remember: ink is made of ashes; it is the remnants of light. All forms hold their opposites, and so there need be no division or conflict. ❧

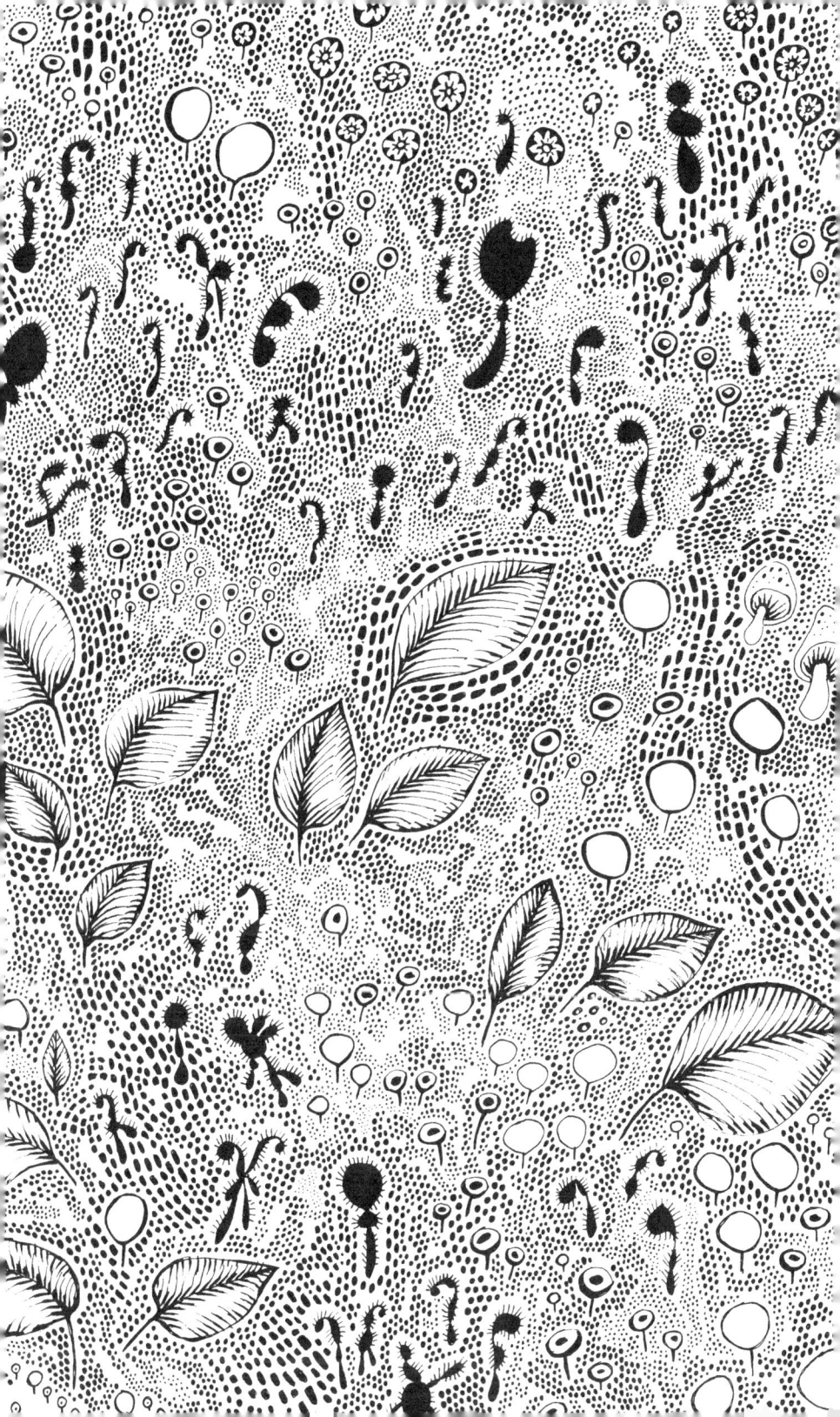

WHY WE OCCUPY
INTERVIEWS BY OLIVIA SCHANZER

How do you structure a movement around radical inclusion? Which past methods have worked? Which methods allow through the cracks forces that will lead to total destabilization? How do you shore up those cracks?

The time in the park was a test kitchen for many ideas, and one can read the following interview with this in mind. Our interviewee, Stefan, was thinking of the movement's big picture as he talked, and he has much to say about it.

Take away from it, certainly, a sense of how little our own plans matter in the face of the greater currents of time, and therefore take away from it a sense of urgency. How can one fully utilize all of the juice present in a movement before it is quashed, or the juice is allowed to drain away? Enthusiasm, excitement and drive are easily expended, and the time of their natural flow is short. Make use of every drop.

Stefan

MY name is Stefan. I'm twenty-two. I live half in the park, half in Brooklyn. I've been here since the beginning.

The first time I was involved with this was in August. I went to one of the first pre-General Assembly meetings, and then I had to take a big step back. I was here day one, and on and off for the first two weeks, but I was recording an album. Then I went on tour for three weeks, so I was kind of being involved, and then cutting out a chunk of the life here. Then I came back three and a half weeks ago or so, if my math serves me well, and have been on the ground, entrenched, pulling, like, twelve plus hours every day since, and that's kind of an indefinite thing.

I do Facilitation and Structure. I help with the tents, as well as a few other side projects here and there, as needed. Generally, just existing here means that you're doing a lot of other work in a lot of other places.

I don't have a real set tent here. I'm just kind of floating around under the good will of others who might have space on the night, you know? It's a tricky process, but I find it's important to sleep here because then I can get to the nine a.m. co-ordinators' meetings. I can be entrenched in the culture of the park, and I can help switch the culture to something that's beneficial and healthy and sustainable, as opposed to just . . . like, it's a little leery right now. Some of the people in the park don't quite have a long-term vision. So I'm just trying to be here, to be an entity that is ready to work in the long haul.

Could you talk about some of the changes you're seeing?

On a physical level, things are very different. It actually looked like a park once upon a time, and the General Assemblies were around one of these potted-plant things. There was, like, two hundred people. It was way tiny, and this whole west side of the park was almost completely empty. It felt weird. It felt like the park was really big at that moment. If you imagine nothing else is in this, this is kind of a large-size park. But now it's completely filled to the brim, literally. We're having police confiscating tents because they're just spilling over into the sidewalk. They're trying their hardest to be in the park, and they can't be here.

When I went away to play music—when I went on tour—before then, there were no tents. And when I came back, all the tents were here. So that was the biggest change, the biggest shock for me. I'm trying to adjust myself to this world, where there are all these tents and the tents are really disorganized. So that's a big one.

Culturally, I've seen a lot of shifts, too. Before I left—and maybe this has to do with the tents—the people who were here were, by and large, either the people who were in it for the long haul, or tourists who wanted to see what was going on. There was no middle ground. And now I see a lot of people on the west side of the park that are involved in their own microcosm of culture. They have their own ways of organizing or not organizing that don't work in tandem with the larger Occupy Wall Street movement—the reason why we have actually come here in the first place.

That's something I've noticed. It started occurring the past month, maybe, and it's a little upsetting because it doesn't help us clarify our vision of why we're here. It doesn't help us think about things in three-month, six-month, year patterns. I don't think that maybe what they want is what we want here. I think what they want is very rooted in the spatial here. Not to create this divide, like us and them, but the people who are in working groups have affinities that are action-oriented, that are radical. We're trying very hard to come together, and that's a difficult process, too.

I have noticed a lot of splintering and fragmentation since I first started here. Before, it was like, "We need to do the things we need to do because they need to be done." We didn't come in with the intention of having a million working groups. They came out of necessity, and I understand that, but now they've all become these little cultures in and of themselves. I just see them rocketing off in their own directions without this consciousness of the whole, and that's really dangerous in terms of collective liberation.

Town Planning can do the best they can to make tents available for everyone, but if we're not—and I'm on Town Planning so that's the reason I'm saying this—but if we're not taking into consideration sexism, racism, homophobia, and real consent policies and things like that—if we're not looking at all of these other things that should be interwoven to all that we do—then we're just building another destructive culture like the one we're fighting against. We're just building a microcosm of the culture we're fighting against, which is really hard for us to get our minds around.

But there's good things happening, too; I don't want to focus on the negative. On a positive end, our allies are coming in full force. We have a ton of people who are providing lots of support. We have people from Egypt coming in. There are trainers from all over the world, sitting down with us to try to tell us these things that are so vital, trainers for forty years that are sitting down and spending weeks on end here, just conferencing with us, trying to drill into our heads how to do this and how to do it well. So that's awesome. We're totally lucky.

It's like going to college for free. Every day, you're just learning from your peers, learning by your actions, learning from mentors and elders who've come in, who can provide resources to you, not to mention the physical resources we have that are almost endless. It feels almost endless, to some degree. I mean, everything has an end, but . . .

There's a lot to offer, there's a lot of potential, and there's a lot of issues. A lot of bridges need to be built, and there are ways to do it, and we'll find out which ones are effective.

I've been running around with my head cut off for a few weeks, and that's an issue. In the past few days, I'm realizing that what we need to be focusing on isn't so much the urgent, but the important. And while we can find things that are both urgent and important, we should be focusing on the important, but not urgent. And that's our vision.

What's the distinction?

An important, not urgent thing would be why we're here in the first place, why we came to this park. Take ourselves out of our context of this park, and look down at what are we doing and what are we building and why we are building it. Those are the important things. What we build in six months isn't urgent, but it's important, and it needs to be talked about now.

The urgent and important are the things that are in this park that we need to address immediately because they directly link in with our views. So if we're splintering as groups, that's urgent and important.

But the urgent non-important are these things that happen day-to-day that we freak out about because we're so entrenched in our own mindset in this park. We're like, "Oh, my God! This person slept in this tent!" or, "This person said this thing!" or, "The police acted in this way today!" as opposed to saying, "How can we get into the mindset of police in relationship to here? How can we get into the mindset of this culture?" The urgent non-important are specific things, and we focus so much of our efforts and time on it that it's exhausting. We're so exhausted, we can't focus on the abstract important things that need to happen, and that's dangerous. But we can overcome these issues.

Last week people were starting to do Spokes Council. Has that been answering the issues at all?

It's been addressing the issues; I don't think it's been answering them yet. Again, people are in this urgent state. As someone in Structure who helps organize the Spokes Council, I know that the Spokes Council is our strongest weapon. It's the best information-sharing warehouse we have. Anyone from any of the operations groups that have been consented upon can share their information with each other. We can pool our abilities together. We can use that as a model to build things. That's awesome. But what we keep seeing is less and less consent, more and more airing of issues that people have. I think that they are urgent issues. However, some of them are important and some aren't.

We are trying to push forward the Spokes Council because we do think it's a model that works. We've been told by many people in many contexts that it does work. We've seen it work in other Occupys. It works in a lot of anti-fracking movements in upstate New York. It worked to end the U.S. invasion of Nicaragua. It worked to end building nuclear plants in the United States. It's done a lot. It's the best information clearinghouse that any radical, non-hierarchical organization could use. It's great, and it's time-honored. So we're not reinventing the wheel. We're just trying to replace a bad wheel with a good wheel.

The Spokes Council, when and if it gets up, will be awesome, but right now, just having everyone in the same room together is volatile.

We have to understand that, and it might take a while for us to air that out before we can sit and really work. A lot of people have issues with each other, and we need to feel out how we can overcome this urgent obstacle to get to the things that are really important in the macro.

Which just leads me to a really quick statement that a lot of people are taking this movement personally, and I think that's very toxic. I think what we need to realize is that when we're here, we're building as parts of this movement, not as our personal selves. We need to take care of our personal bodies and our needs, but those can happen both in the park and outside of the park. People should feel welcome to take a step back for a night or two and just decompress, get their head straight, as opposed to throwing their needs out to the movement. That gets very heavy and very crazy. And personal arguments need not happen here. They can happen elsewhere. This needs to be a space for the movement to build and grow.

Do you think that's the answer to defusing tension? People taking better care of themselves?

Yeah, I think that that's a huge part of it. If we take care of our needs, then we impose a lot less on other people, and we have a better focus and sense of self. One of the skill sets that I've been learning here a lot is nonviolent communication, which just says that if we recognize our needs, and recognize that we're the only people who can satisfy our needs, then we can be a lot less detrimental to other people and to ourselves. I think that it's good to have Wellness, N.V.C., De-Escalation, lots of people on-site to help with that, but it's also personal accountability and self-facilitation.

There is one day when I first came back here that I just wasn't eating or drinking, and I was working a lot. And then I wound up snapping at someone. The second that I did that, I pulled back and said, "Wait a minute! Red flag! I'm not taking care of my body. I'm not taking care of myself, and because of that, I'm starting to be detrimental to other people. I'm going home tonight. I'm going to cook a big breakfast in the morning, and I'm going to pack a lunch, and I'm bringing water. I'm going to fix this right now, before I dig this hole," you know? I think, if we all recognize where we are at physically and mentally and spiritually, then we can create this system that's better.

I understand that not everyone can go back to an apartment, but we're slowly building up an infrastructure of people who have spaces and can offer them. I'm trying to pass along the information that several people from upstate New York have offered log cabins for anyone to go up to for retreats.

That's really nice.

There's a whole network of support all over the world that's willing to take care of us and get into a headspace where we can push and build, but we have to be accepting. We have to be accepting of the fact that we, as individuals, need space from this park sometimes.

But as a movement, we need to focus on what's important.

Could you explain to me a little bit about how Structure works?

Well, what Structure does right now is mostly focused on the Spokes Council. We do some of the spatial stuff, like, we try to get the actual spaces for Spokes Council. We send out the emails to all the working groups, letting everyone know where the Spokes Councils are, what time they are, because the times fluctuate a little bit. They're usually seven to ten or seven thirty to ten thirty, but that really depends on the space and their needs, so it fluctuates.

Also, it's kind of a very intense brainstorming session for how we're going to try to set the spokes. We had, like, an eight-hour conversation one day just about, "How are we going to get the spokes consented upon?" because that's not the G.A. process. That's not the traditional consent process. How can we do it in a way where everyone is validated, recognized, and there's reducing the amount of back-and-forth for personal conversations and personal arguments to come in?

We want: "Is this group an operations group? Yes? Or does it need further discussion?" And if it's, "Yes, they're consented upon," that's it. We can flesh out personal grievances or tactical issues later, but we have to get these groups in now. There are other spaces and forums to handle these grievances. You can come to these working groups and say, "Hey, I think you're having these major issues in these ways, and we need to talk about it." I think that there should be other forums for this, and that's maybe a piece of the puzzle that hasn't been fleshed out as much but needs to happen more.

How many working groups are ideally involved in Spokes Council? All of them?

It's operations working groups, and I can't speak on how many because that's not up for me to decide, but it's any group that logistically or financially contributes to the operations of Liberty Park. That's what we are building here.

Okay. So Comfort, Library . . .

Yeah. I'm trying to think of who's already been in. Medic is in. Sanitation is in. Kitchen is in. I think N.V.C. is in. I think Comfort is in. Finance is

in. Anyone who's handling the tactical everydays—those people are the ones that we're mostly talking about.

There are other groups that might get in, like Facilitation and Training—things that do provide services, but maybe it's slightly more up for debate whether they're operational or logistical. And then there's groups that a lot of people want to discuss because we're not sure. A lot of those might be movement groups.

Also, note that caucuses are welcome, caucuses being a body of people who have a common affinity, usually around marginalization. So there's a women's caucus,[1] there's a People of Color Caucus, there's a Queering O.W.S. caucus ... the women haven't quite found their way in yet. Every time they're ready to speak, something goes wrong in the Spokes Council, and the Spokes Council deflates.

Wow, that is so horrifyingly true-to-life.

I feel so bad. To take off the Structure hat for a second: We really, really need the women's caucus in.

That really bums me out, I have to say.

Yeah, it bums me out, too. It's really important that they're there. I think that the caucuses are really healthy in these Spokes Councils. The caucuses are threading into these meetings that which is really important to

---

[1] Women Occupying Wall Street (WOW).

all of us. So when a group acts in a sexist way, the women's caucus can say, "I'm standing up and I'm going to directly address this." It's great to have a forum. Like, "This spoke will handle these issues. And while we all can feel empowered to deal with them, this spoke has a lot of knowledge about this, really understands the issues, and can speak concisely on it so that we're not all going back and forth."

The models that work the best are: Small groups with common affinities get most of the shit done. Then bring in larger groups, like a Spokes Council, to share information and to draw more people to those affinities. We're here as autonomous collectives. Occupy Wall Street is a movement, but each group should be entitled to make its own decisions. I can't tell the kitchen what kind of food to get or how to organize their structure or when their hours are. I accept the fact that they are based on what's best for them because they have a much better knowledge, in the same way that I don't complain to Medic about what kind of medicine they have or how they practice it. But if there's a serious issue that could compromise the movement, then we can discuss it. There are working groups that might have these larger issues, but by and large, we need to respect autonomy of working groups. These larger movements, like the General Assembly and Spokes Councils and things like this, should really just be information-clearing and asking for things that are larger than themselves.

What is a General Assembly issue versus a Spokes Council issue?

Once we have the Spokes Council in place, the Spokes Council will handle all financial things that are operational to the movement. General Assemblies, we are trying to have more of an open invitation for people to brainstorm and popcorn—which is a style of brainstorming session where anyone just calls out things— or breakout groups about ideas, theories. Like, "We want to talk today about our relationship with the neighborhood." Or, "We want to talk about Occupy Wall Street in relation to the other Occupys." Or, "What are we, as the Occupy movement, doing in this macro picture? Let's just talk about it." They could have breakout groups and small information, and then harvest it and bring it back to this wider community. That's really healthy because that's a way for us to be self-aware. So that's what I think a General Assembly is good for. And that should be open to anyone and all people.

I do think a Spokes Council should be open, but the most important people in the Spokes Council are the spokes themselves, conferring with the other spokes. If all the spokes are there, legitimately speaking on behalf of their working groups, I think that that would be an acceptable Spokes Council to me. I do like having other people from working groups come in to back their spokes, so that they can confer with each other on issues that they might not have addressed in their internal working groups. I think it's healthy. But it's not an open meeting for tourists and for people . . . like, you can audit it if there's space, and I'd love to find a large enough space for that, but we do have to accept the reality that we are in Lower Manhattan. There aren't five-hundred, six-hundred-person meeting spaces that are friendly with Occupy Wall Street and available in two days at a price we can afford.

You guys have to rent space for it?

Yep.

What kind of spaces are you getting?

Well, we were in a high school cafeteria over by the Brooklyn Bridge for two days.

Oh, were you in Murry Bergtraum? I used to teach there.

I think it was. It's right by the police precinct?

Yeah. I know that cafeteria well.

It was very hot.

It's unpleasant.

Yep, didn't create the best atmosphere.

But I think Murry Bergtraum, the guy whom it was named after, was some sort of old-school socialist.[2]

Cool. Maybe that's one of the reasons they were down for us.

Then we were at a really nice area, although it was a little bit too small. We were at a Trinity Church reception area that fit two-twenty people. We had about three hundred people in the space, and they were still letting people in and out. They weren't harassing us about it. They were really actually really, really awesome and welcoming. But there was some controversy about Structure putting out this email to everyone, asking each working group to only bring, like, three or four people backing up the spoke. That isn't super all-inclusive.

Isn't the spoke rotating?

Yeah.

So I mean, they'll be included eventually, right?

Yeah, and I think that's fine. The spoke has to rotate every time. It keeps working groups of one—which do exist here—it keeps them from being able to be present at the meetings, because you're not a working

---

[2] Murry Bergtraum (1916–1973) was an accountant for the fur industry who presided over the New York City Board of Education in 1970–71.

group of one. That's not a working group. That's not even a group. To take us out of Occupy Wall Street world and into the dictionary, that's not a group. The dictionary will argue that this group has no validity in this space. It's not a personal bias, it's kind of an objective thing.

How many working groups of one are there?

I think two, maybe three.

I'm not going to ask what they are.

I'm not going to tell.

No, no. Keep moving.

So the Spokes Council is here for information-clearing, because no one has time to sit in on every group. I have no clue what goes on in the groups that I'm not involved with. It's like blind spots in my vision, you know? I can see where Structure is. I can see the future of Facilitation. I can see where the tents are now, and where the tents will be in the future, hopefully. And I can also see some of the larger "where we as a movement are going," just because I'm involved with a lot of the network here. But I have no idea what's going to happen with a lot of these groups. Being able to sit in on the Spokes Council is awesome. It's really empowering.

What would you say is the direction now?

I'm not completely sure, but what I see is us transcending this physical space. We need to, and we need to soon. And although we never know where we are, I'd like to see us really fleshing out what's important to us, networking with other people who've already been doing it, and doing it a long time. Kind of going glacial, in many ways, although still maintaining this really strong vibe. Having really good campaigns, like, "We're going to shut down this!" in a spirit of direct action, while also being an entity in our community, and taking this model and bringing it to other places. So it's not about ... I don't know how to describe it ... I think physical occupation is really good because it is a clearinghouse for information; it roots us in the spatial, it's symbolic, it's theatrical. But what I see is our ideas going forth.

As an occupier, I'd like to see a lot less government, a lot less corporatization. Mostly, I just want to see people feel empowered, and empowering themselves.

What we're doing here isn't a reactionary movement. That's why we don't have demands. We're here because we're a non-hierarchical community-building movement. We're testing out how communities can get together, and if we can find a way that works, that's going to go everywhere. That's going to spread like wildfire, and it already is, to some degree. That's why everyone is talking about consensus, and I couldn't be happier. If we're talking about consensus, then we should be talking about consent—personal consent—and if we can all take in personal consent, we're going to be much healthier.

How are you distinguishing between consensus and consent?

Consent is a personal thing. I can consent to this interview. Occupy Wall Street doesn't need to consent to me having this interview because it respects that I'm an autonomous individual with decisions. Consent is an individual saying yes to something. It always comes into it in terms of sexuality, but a good consent policy applies to everything that we do in our lives. It's being held personally accountable to make decisions, and then empowering ourselves to vocalize those decisions so that we're not put in situations that we don't want to be in—we're not put in these coercive combinations, as Utah Phillips would say.

Consensus is: As a movement, as a body of people, we all agree this is something that can happen. So consensus is a large-scale thing, a way of groups deciding things. Consensus is the idea that we don't have to take votes. We don't have to marginalize people and step over people in our way of progress.

Which is happening, and we do need to be aware of that as an issue. That's part of the urgent and not important. We need to consent to things as a movement, and we need to feel empowered horizontally to speak up, to raise issues, to raise questions and concerns. And also, we need to know that just because someone has an idea that we may not agree with fully, we should be respecting its autonomy unless we really feel like it's compromising us as a whole. Consensus is an individual speaking on behalf of a part of the movement, as an entity of the movement.

How do you empower people in the greater world toward an ability to consent?

The biggest way it seems to be happening is just by everyone being plugged into what's going on here and watching. Watching us in the media and coming to the park and just seeing everything that we've built here. We've built a lot, and it's very impressive. We should celebrate the victories that we've already accomplished.

I think that people want that world that we want. It's a pretty common idea. We want that world, and we're providing a model. Whether that model's perfect or not . . . it's certainly not, but I think it could be really good. And we're still building it, so it's a work in progress. But we're providing a rubric for people to base their own community on, and that's really cool.

Everyone comes to Facilitation

meetings and says, "We're from all these other Occupys. You need to help us." We're not, like, the parent occupation, but it feels like we are, and we do have to take that in the back of our minds. In all that we do, the whole world is watching us. Not just the media and all these people, but all the other occupations, all the other activist movements.

And we're looking to Greece, looking to Spain, looking to Egypt in the same way that they're looking back at us. We're learning from each other. In this consensus model, we're both saying yes to our movement-building, and we respect the autonomy of the other one. We can't have the same tactics that Greece has; it doesn't work here. But we can learn from the Greek model.

I've spoken to a lot of people from other Occupys who told me that they came here to learn what's going on, and are taking it back home with them.

I hope that they're sharing what they've learned, too, because that's the other part of it. I just hope, because we're looking to other Occupys for certain models ourselves.

What are you learning from the other Occupys?

Some already have effective Spokes Councils. Some know how to handle destructive, toxic people in ways that we don't know.

What are some of the ways?

There are evictions in some parks. If someone is time after time disruptive and dangerous to themselves and to others around them, there are people who've been asked to leave and forced to leave. Years ago, I would have thought that was a horrible thing. Now, I don't think it's a horrible thing; I think it's a necessary thing. I feel really bad saying that because it doesn't create this air of all-inclusiveness, but if you're a danger to yourself and to the others around you, there's no justification that these people should be here, especially if other avenues have already been explored.

It's a very dangerous route because it's hard. People want everyone to be here, and I want everyone to be here, but we have to take care of our needs. If we're not taking care of our needs, that's really detrimental to everyone around us, including ourselves. That's really dangerous. We need to build the safest space possible for ourselves and for the world. It's hard.

It's very exciting at the same time.

Yeah. I'm nervous and optimistic, working really hard, and trying to not just spin my wheels when I'm working, which takes perspective, too. That's my personal challenge right now is: How can I be more efficient and doing less busy work? ℘

Congratulations!
You're part of the problem!

Were you among that group of city dwellers who avoided the park at Wall Street in 2011 because of your abhorrence of homeless individuals?

Are you the sort who turns up your nose at crusty punks?

Did you think that that was the only sort of person who was down at Liberty Plaza? And if it had been, would you consider questioning your preconceptions about the worth of human individuals? No? Oy, for Pete's sake!

Well, now look what you bought yourself! You might have redeemed your politics five years ago, but instead, by ignoring what was going on, you have a demagogue for a president and a nation of disenfranchised and angry people. Couldn't we have done something to stop this then?

Buy this book and
try to get a grip on yourself!

http://www.matchlock.com

SUBWAY SKETCHBOOK

BY AGIR

To Land a Man

A novel by
Olivia Schanzer

IV

Thoughts of a happy match colored the whole of Mrs Wallace's mundane errands the following morning. She had extracted from Henry the promise that he would come again to dinner in order to meet her daughter, and even the onerous trip to the bank was made less so by her pleasant thoughts. Her bank, which had once been a pillared refuge, had now swapped silence for din, cool for overheating, and a timely attendance to one's needs for a surfeit of speed or much too long a wait. Mrs Wallace had seen the security guard there ask an elderly lady to get up from her seat because she was in the area where one waited for loans and she was not waiting for a loan. The elderly lady was not a bag person, either, and had merely sat down to catch her breath, of which she did not have enough to take the security guard to task.

Despite how they wished to hurry one along, Mrs Wallace would not fondle screens while being hurried, and so she waited in line, sat down to talk with an unhelpful woman behind a particle-board desk—perhaps, Mrs Wallace always considered, Katherine would have preferred it to the battered secretary Mrs Wallace kept in the corner of the study—and left again, remembering fondly the days of bank books, and her mother's favorite teller, Marguerite, with whom she would talk of marriage while she made her deposits.

In the afternoon, Mrs Wallace had a meeting with her lawyer, an errand in stark opposition to that trip to the bank. Mrs Wallace's lawyer was as knowledgeable and invested in her life and family history as anyone outside of her immediate relatives, indeed more than some of those. He was of the oldest school, had worked for her father before her, and could be called on to supply, in addition to legal counsel, all types of other counsel as well, whether it was solicited or not. In fact, it was more a question of stopping up his counsel, as it flowed freely and in every direction. Mrs Wallace's father had always enjoyed his company, and had seen him socially, as well. Mrs Wallace, though never as close to him as her father had been, for reasons of gender, had always found his dark wit and paternalism engaging.

But Mr Desmond had changed a bit over the years. This was, of course, an inevitability of life. Experience was proprietary, Mrs Wallace knew, and it did not loosen its grip on one's sensibilities to allow one to return to innocence and old forms. The changes in Mr Desmond, however, went beyond those all people faced. As she remembered him from his youth, when he was in her father's employ, he had been an energetic, neatly presentable and striving upstart at his firm, and he had continued to grow steadily in stature, both personal and professional, over the years. This man she had known, however, the one whose immaculate handkerchief protruded from a well-pressed and well-cut suit from Hong Kong, was nowhere now to be found.

The change had been so gradual that she had perhaps not noticed its grave progression. Clearly he had been something close to his old self fifteen years ago, when he had handled the wills of her parents with great tact and acumen. At that time, perhaps, he had already begun to wear a sport coat of somewhat reduced quality—though, she imagined, not the type with gold buttons from off the rack—and had ceased to wear the Italian socks that matched his immaculate handkerchief; one viewed them with pleasure when he crossed his legs. The sport-coat phase lasted many years, and Mrs Wallace had had no professional objections to this slight informality, even if she might have had personal.

Of late a turn had been taken, and Mrs Wallace noticed it with increasing alarm. She believed her memories of him to be exact, yet clearly they could not be, for the man she was faced with now—the man who was in charge of her family's personal business, complaints, issues of proprietary right and the like—could not be the outgrowth of that previous one, who radiated such sharp intelligence that the tap of an unlit Chesterfield upon his gold cigarette case was rhetoric enough to dispense with his adversaries. Mr Desmond, if she were polite in her phrasing, was not improving. It was not only his clothes, but his affect, his use of language, his overall presentation—so important in a lawyer, even one who does not stand up at trials—that had seemed to deteriorate. In fact, she was forced to admit that this downhill roll was nearing that point at which he would teeter off the cliff, taking with him all of her business affairs. If she wished to save herself, the only proper thing to do was to bite down hard and fire him.

Yet there were several private

things that kept Mrs Wallace from doing so, even if it had already come to the point where propriety demanded it. The first was that, though he no longer worked for her, Mr Desmond had spent many of the last thirty years in the employ of Mrs Chester. This was a woman from whose house privileged information sometimes flowed, but trustworthy analysis was not readily available.

Mr Desmond had refused to take on Mrs Chester's case against Landmarks, and because of this, the two had severed their acquaintance. Mrs Chester had hired on, instead of Mr Desmond, her own son, who did not know enough of the law to approve or disapprove an instance of its use. Of course, then, and by his own volition, Mr Desmond himself was now a loyal enemy of Mrs Chester.

"I do not naturally take moral affront," he had told Mrs Wallace at the time, "but here I make an exception."

Beyond this, there was even a further reason for Mrs Wallace's attachment: the fact that Mr Desmond handled the legal affairs of her own daughter. This confounded Mrs Wallace's resolve against him irreparably, for, though she might have done without his opinions on Mrs Chester, Mr Desmond saw it as part of his job to inform on Katherine to Mrs Wallace whenever the slightest thing of interest occurred. In a different generation, this had always been the job of the family lawyer, and Mr Desmond was most conscientious about it.

Katherine had come into a little money of her own, and this was the main ore that Mr Desmond mined for Mrs Wallace, for as trustee, he was the one consulted when money was removed (having been appointed by a relative of Katherine's who trusted no one related to the Wallaces with the job), and he could even—and Katherine still did not understand why this should be—tell her when and if the money could be extracted at all.

Mrs Wallace and Mr Desmond were bound the tighter the more Mr Desmond seemed to disintegrate, for her daughter seemed to feel fonder of him the worse he got. The more Mr Desmond's appearance suggested he stood ardently against the hoarding of capital, the more Katherine confided in him. With all this in mind, this meeting, as her meetings with him always were, was fraught with purpose.

The building where Mr Desmond had his office was—as would be expected from a respectable lawyer, though not from the man he was now—elegant and well-situated. The stream of people who moved through the lobby gave proof to the idea that the rents were very high, for no one passed, Mrs Wallace noted, who was not wearing good shoes.

In the bright afternoon sun, the lobby of the office building glinted fiercely, and Mrs Wallace found herself shading her eyes from the glare as she walked to the front desk. There was a strange inlay of gold on one whole wall, abstract and many-layered, which she had seen many times, but at which she had never looked. Now, as she entered the lobby, she was blinded by it, for the sun was hitting it directly.

"Have you got the time of your appointment right?" the man at the desk asked her. He had called up to Mr Desmond's office, but Mr Desmond had not answered. Mrs Wallace, who did not get times wrong for appointments, scowled at him and said, "Continue ringing and I will wait." Mr Desmond's secretary, she supposed, had been given the morning off, as she seemed to have been for the last one hundred mornings in recent memory. Mr Desmond now appeared to answer, or fail to answer, his own phone.

She turned a displeased eye again upon the gilded wall. She moved to an angle where the glare was less potent, and examined it. It looked most like an enormous topographic map, and it was traversed along all its odd, jutting masses by pinpricks.

It brought to mind, in all its golden peaks and golden valleys, the dowry with which Indian girls were married. If only all the components of an American dowry appreciated. The most important one certainly did not, and that was one's maidenhead, or if one were to be less coarse, the fact of being a maiden, young and desirable. But this piece said something else as well. The pinpricks reminded her of those she had seen in Churchill's map, the movements of supplies between the Allies. Here, too, in the world beyond war, supplies changed hands. Ardor given was turned with the exchange of vows to material assets. Finances were repositioned: a summer house, stocks, savings accounts. She looked at the name plate beside it: *The Ebb and Flow of Commerce*.

"Sir," she asked the man at the front desk, who seemed to stand somber guard over that display. "Is that piece gold-plated? The gold could not possibly be solid." She gestured towards the wall.

The man leaned in and beckoned her closer with a finger. He had the air of a man long awaiting this particular moment of conspiracy. "It is a very thin patina. And do you know the price tag for such a work? Can you guess?" As its sole curator, perhaps its only advocate, he was eager to discuss it. Mrs Wallace did not volunteer an answer.

"Two and a half million. It seems a lot, but Madame, for all its worth, if you take your thumbnail to it, the gold flakes off easily," and he made a chipping motion in the direction of the wall. "By the time I have retired, I will have done my best with this one finger nail to ruin the entire wall." Whether this was a monstrous act, or one quite clever and deserved, Mrs Wallace could not tell, and so she made no return at all to that anarchic doorman. Most likely, he would not have too much luck ruining it, working at the pace he was going, though he was on the young side and still had many years to go before retirement.

The elevator doors opened now, and Mr Desmond came out into the lobby, a plastic bag in one hand. "Like a homeless," Mrs Wallace remarked to herself, still contemplating the doorman's life project. Mr Desmond was dressed in old, filthy jeans and the kind of sport coat that might have been popular for a tweedy professor a long time ago. He was wearing on top of the outfit a long, moth-eaten cashmere scarf which had clearly belonged to better times. Mrs Wallace, who did not consider herself easily shockable, found herself inhaling quickly when she pictured this man in control of many of the family's assets.

Mr Desmond nodded awkwardly to the doorman, and hardly making contact with Mrs Wallace or acknowledging her beyond a small wave, he handed the little bundle of trash he was holding to that man, and ushered Mrs Wallace back into the elevator. "It is so nice of you to come," he said, only after the doors closed and they were alone together. She wondered where he had been that kept him from answering his phone for so long, but thought better of asking.

Despite whatever was the ailment of its keeper, Mr Desmond's office had somehow withstood his internal turbulence, and it remained tidy and soothing to the eye. This, of course, made his own dishevelment all the more jarring in contrast; there he stood, for all the world a homeless who had wandered into a well-run workplace.

"Would you like a cup of coffee or tea, Mrs Wallace?" he asked genteelly. Mrs Wallace declined, imagining the sight of Mr Desmond's browned fingernails steadying the rim as the drink made its way to her.

"How are you feeling, Mr Desmond? Were you able to take a holiday this summer?" she asked with what she hoped was fitting significance.

"I'm quite well, quite well. But no holiday, Mrs Wallace. You know I think of work as a holiday. Work is the holiday from myself."

"Not even a weekend at the beach?"

Mr Desmond laughed but did not reply.

"What about you? Did you have a good summer?"

Mrs Wallace said she had.

There were papers to look over, and Mrs Wallace looked them over critically; she was eager to analyze his shaky handwriting to see if she might discern there any sign of excessive weakness beyond the bodily. She was no lawyer, but the papers seemed fine.

"Well," she said, finally looking up. "Any word from Katherine?" Mr Desmond sat for a moment in reflection, trying to recall.

"I saw her just this past week. She brought along that gray man she carries with her. I hoped for your sake you might have nipped it in the bud already, but you do not seem to wish it. Once we would have snipped, snipped, snipped," he said sadly with his fingers held high, clipping the air, "but now perhaps you must just stand it. If you don't mind me saying, I am very sorry to see you stand it."

"I do not stand it," said Mrs Wallace who had come here for advice and information, and now felt sorry to be burdened with either one. "I have no intention of standing it. If you have lost sleep over my standing it, be assured, I do not stand it."

"She has mentioned several times her happiness with Doug when I inquired not at all about it. 'Mr Desmond, I am sublimely happy with him. I cannot tell you how glad I am to have found a man like that.' I'm sure she intended me to pass it on."

Mrs Wallace sighed impatiently.

"I see you are passing it on, my good Mr Desmond; you have just yourself passed it on." Mr Desmond conceded that that was the case.

"She said to me, 'I will marry him as soon as I can. We only just wait for his fortunes to turn, as he is low presently. One does not like to waste such a happy day, when the principal party is so blue!'" As Mr

Desmond talked he took on, most strangely to Mrs Wallace, Katherine's own affect. Though his stubble and wide shoulders were his own, he seemed to have become that girl for a moment or two. Katherine in absentia seemed as wicked and resistant to Mrs Wallace as Katherine present always did, and she longed, as she did when faced with that sober, recalcitrant face, to shout something out, perhaps to slap her, but here, too, when faced with only her shadow, she held her tongue.

"She believes she is quite committed to him," Mrs Wallace said. "I have never thought that the commitment is true."

"She said, 'Nothing will draw us asunder as long as I have any will,'" said Mr Desmond, with the firm quivering lip her daughter often generated.

"She will not say that to me, of course. Only to you. Nevertheless," said Mrs Wallace to her simulacrum daughter, who sat and looked intently at her, and who had not removed his moth-eaten scarf—she imagined he must be chilled, and felt sorry—"I intend to draw them asunder."

"Yes," said Mr Desmond, now himself, "It is only right that the mother have a say."

"There is a very fine man afoot," said Mrs Wallace. "He will be coming to my house this week, and Katherine has agreed to come as well."

"If you will allow me the impertinence," Mr Desmond said to Mrs Wallace, who nodded. She did not mind it especially from Mr Desmond, who had, for many years, supplied her own father with that quality, and whom she visited, in part, to receive her own measure of it.

"When I was a young man, there was a father at my firm with the very same problem as the one you have. The very same problem: Love was professed frequently there, too, and the father also vowed to split apart his daughter and her beau. I was there in the coffee room when he made that vow, and he did do it!"

"How did he accomplish it?" Mrs Wallace asked, genuinely interested.

"Just as you intend, with a very fine man who worked at that firm. He too was afoot. The father invited him over to his house one Saturday afternoon—the daughter and her sub-par young man had a date—and he arrived into the living room when the two were sitting there together upon the sofa, quite content." Mr Desmond looked at

Mrs Wallace, and she gestured to him that he should go on.

"Upon the first beau's pale summer suit the second beau spilled his coffee, though he was on all usual occasions quite nimble. The spill had been contracted, of course, by the father. It had the necessary effect, for the daughter was taken out that afternoon by the man who had spilt, instead of the first man. The man who had been spilt upon returned home to change his suit!"

"Is that the case? And what happened with that couple?"

"When the young woman saw how courteously behaved the spiller, and how discourteously behaved the man upon whom that coffee was spilt, her heart was swayed, and for several seasons she and the spiller saw each other exclusively," said Mr Desmond. "Must I spell out for you the moral, Mrs Wallace? I offer you some very practical advice!" And he looked at her with glee. "Of course, Mrs Wallace, I was the young man who spilt! Though I never had any true intentions regarding that man's daughter, I was happy to help, out of a pure sense of loyalty." Mr Desmond here paused.

"I tell you, Mrs Wallace, that it is not natural for me to hate Doug. I do not even know him except for what I've seen in the waiting room. It is a testament to my loyalty to you and your father that I do so. Doug has even sent business my way."

"I thought you weren't taking any new clients. What has happened to your retirement?" She looked at his strange appearance and wondered over the person who would hire Mr Desmond knowing only this side of him.

Mr Desmond shrugged, but did not reply to the question. "Mrs Wallace, I probably will not live long enough to see the full fruits of the seeds of your malice, but I remain faithful to you until the last. If you ever need my assistance, or the use of my name could help you in any way, do not hesitate to ask for it. It is my supreme pleasure to assist. However, anything you do, I prefer it to cut really to the quick, especially if my name is on it. The young are only capable of inflicting surface wounds these days, and that I cannot respect.

"Nevertheless," he said, now changing his tone to one of pure professionalism, for he had grown very strange as he talked, and very far away, "her spending is not too extreme, you'll be happy to know, and she has asked for no extra money. She appears to be living on her salary, though not particularly well. That is all we have, Mrs Wallace," her lawyer said to her, as if he had been cycling through company reports rather than planning a coup and, as she was sure Katherine would phrase it, tattling.

"I am glad to hear your opinion about Katherine," Mrs Wallace said, rising to shake Mr Desmond's hand.

Mr Desmond now leaned down to tie his shoelace, which he had only now realized was untied, even though he had walked to the lobby with it in that condition and nearly tripped several times.

"Mr Desmond," Mrs Wallace remarked as she was leaving because she could not resist, "Where are all the fine suits you used to wear?"

Mr Desmond smiled, and she could see, although she was not quite sure of it, that he appeared to be missing an eye tooth. "They weren't very comfortable," he replied. "Surely as a woman you can understand the desire to be more comfortable." ℰ

Meet the BEST ping pong player on Sobek!

Read all about Fmr. Ambassador Qui-deeé in the pages of
"Homesick for Earth" by Olivia Schanzer

Visit Matchlock Press at
http://www.matchlock.com

IT'S NO SURPRISE THAT THE GAP IN OUR APPREHENSION OF THE FACTS HAS BEEN FILLED BY THE MOST FANTASTIC INVENTIONS OF OUR LITERARY FOREBEARS.

THAT **SOMETHING** HAPPENED COULD NOT BE MORE EVIDENT.

A SHIP SET OUT ON A VOYAGE, AND THEN . . .

WE WILL ENGAGE IN SOME SUCH SPECULATION THIS EVENING, BUT WE WILL TRY TO DO SO IN AN INFORMED FASHION, WITH THE HELP OF A QUALIFIED GUIDE.

MY GUEST IS A RELUCTANT GHOST HUNTER WHOSE USUAL BEAT COVERS THE MOST MUNDANE OF AREAS: CARGO, TRAFFIC, LOGISTICS.

HE'S THE HARBORMASTER OF CORONISPORT.

PLEASE WELCOME CAPTAIN CHANDRAJIT BATRA.

THE LAST THREE HARBORMASTERS WERE ALL FORMER NAVAL OFFICERS, BUT YOU ARE NOT A MILITARY MAN.

NO, I'M NOT.

I COME FROM A LONG LINE OF INDUSTRIALISTS.

MY FAMILY IN CLEEIA MANUFACTURES GRAVITATIONAL FIELD CONDENSERS.

BUT YOU BECAME A SAILOR, INSTEAD.

THAT WAS MY PARTICULAR OBSESSION.

I HAVE PLENTY OF BROTHERS AND SISTERS AND COUSINS WHO ALL WANTED A PIECE OF THE ACTION.

I WAS ENCOURAGED TO GO MY OWN WAY.

"EYES IN THE ETHER" IS THE WATCHWORD FROM THE FAMILY PLAYBOOK.

I TRAINED AT THE MERCHANT MARINE ACADEMY, AND I SERVED FOR MANY YEARS ABOARD THE SHIPS OF THE FAMILY FLEET.

BUT BEING A STARSHIP CAPTAIN TAKES A TOLL ON YOU AFTER A WHILE.

ALAS.

HOW DID YOU END END UP HERE IN CORONISPORT?

IT WAS A FREQUENT PORT OF CALL.

AND I WAS FRIENDS WITH CHRISTIAN BURCHFIELD, WHO WAS GOVERNOR OF CORONISPORT WHEN I WAS APPROACHING RETIREMENT.

HE OFFERED ME THE POST, AND IT SEEMED LIKE A GOOD FIT.

IN FACT, I DO BELIEVE IT SUITS ME WELL.

FORGIVE ME FOR ASKING, BUT WHAT DOES THE HARBORMASTER DO?

IT'S NOT SO MUCH WHAT WE DO AS WHAT WE REPRESENT.

A STAR SYSTEM IS A MAELSTROM OF PLANETS, MOONS, COMETS, ASTEROIDS AND SPACE VESSELS.

ACCIDENTS HAPPEN, DISPUTES FLARE, THE POTENTIAL FOR CHAOS IS VERY HIGH.

WHATEVER WEIRD THING MAY HAPPEN, THE HARBORMASTER'S JOB IS TO **ASSUME RESPONSIBILITY** FOR IT.

TO **OWN** IT, IF YOU WILL.

THAT'S A UNIQUELY PASSIVE THEORY OF LEADERSHIP.

JUST UNIQUELY HONEST, I'M AFRAID.

WE KEEP BUSY, OF COURSE.

BUT IN A WELL-RUN ORGANIZATION, THERE SHOULD BE NO TASK THAT CAN ONLY BE COMPLETED BY THE BOSS.

THIS JOURNEY WAS FRAUGHT WITH RISK FROM THE VERY BEGINNING.

WHOEVER THEY WERE, THEY WERE EITHER BRAVE, DESPERATE, OR UNLUCKY.

BY THE TIME IT REACHED OUR SHORES, THE SHIP HAD GONE COLD. COMPLETELY COLD AND LIFELESS.

NO TRANSMISSIONS, NO HEAT, NOT A SINGLE PHOTON EMANATED FROM THE HULL.

AND IT "DRIFTED" THROUGH AT A MERE TWENTY-TWO HUNDRED KILOMETERS PER SECOND.

IT WAS FIRST CAUGHT BY A RADAR STATION IN THE EARLY WARNING NET, WHEN IT WAS ALREADY ON ITS WAY **OUT** OF THE SYSTEM.

BUT THIS IS ALL STUFF THAT YOU DISCOVERED **AFTER** YOU HAD A CHANCE TO THOROUGHLY EXAMINE THE SHIP.

THAT'S RIGHT.

WHAT ABOUT BEFORE?

OH, NO NO NO!

WE WERE COMPLETELY IN THE DARK!

NOT ONLY THAT, BUT ONCE WE FINALLY GOT IT INTO PORT, NOBODY WANTED TO GO ABOARD!

WHY NOT?

NOW, SEE, HERE'S WHERE I DON'T WANT TO MISREPRESENT ANYONE.

THERE WAS A KIND OF COLLECTIVE DREAD THAT BEFELL US.

LIFELONG SPACEFARING RATIONALISTS WERE SUDDENLY OVERCOME BY SUPERSTITION.

A LIVELY DEBATE ERUPTED OVER WHICH WOULD BE WORSE: FINDING HUMAN REMAINS OR FINDING NOTHING AT ALL.

EVEN THOUGH THERE WAS NO GORE, JUST CLEAN, DRY BONE, THERE'S SOMETHING ABOUT A SKELETON STILL WEARING ITS LAST CHANGE OF CLOTHES THAT HITS YOU RIGHT IN THE ANIMAL PART OF YOUR BRAIN.

WHERE DID THEY COME FROM?

UNFORTUNATELY, THEIR COMPUTER SUFFERED GRAVE DAMAGE DURING THE JOURNEY.

PROBABLY DUE TO COSMIC RAY BOMBARDMENT IN THE INTERSTELLAR MEDIUM.

LUCKILY FOR US, THEIR HEADING STRONGLY SUGGESTED THEIR LIKELY POINT OF ORIGIN.

THE WONDERFUL ARCHIVISTS AT THE MUSEUM OF HUMAN EXPANSION HELPED US SIFT THROUGH THE RECORDS OF THE MANY INDEPENDENT EXPEDITIONS TO THIS PART OF SPACE IN THE EARLY EXPANSION PERIOD.

A SEPARATIST COLONY CALLED "EUTOPIA" WAS SITUATED ABOUT TEN LIGHT-YEARS TO SPINWARD OVER A K-TYPE STAR WHICH IS NOT A MEMBER OF THE HYADES.

FASCINATING!

HAVE YOU SENT WORD?

YES, BUT THERE MAY BE NOBODY THERE TO RECEIVE IT.

AS I SAID, THEY WERE FLYING A SHORT-RANGE VESSEL.

THEY DID **NOT** INTEND TO COME HERE, I'M SURE OF IT.

WE THINK THEY WERE USING OUR STAR AS A NAVIGATIONAL AID WHEN THEIR LIFE SUPPORT FAILED.

SK

EVERYONE ON BOARD WAS KILLED AT THEIR STATIONS BY TOXIC GASES FROM THE HOLD.

THE SHIP CONTINUED TO ACCELERATE FOR A TIME UNTIL IT RAN OUT OF FUEL.

THEN IT SUCCUMBED TO INERTIA, AS ALL BALLISTIC OBJECTS MUST.

BRAIN FEVER NUMBER 4

Ballpoint Perps!

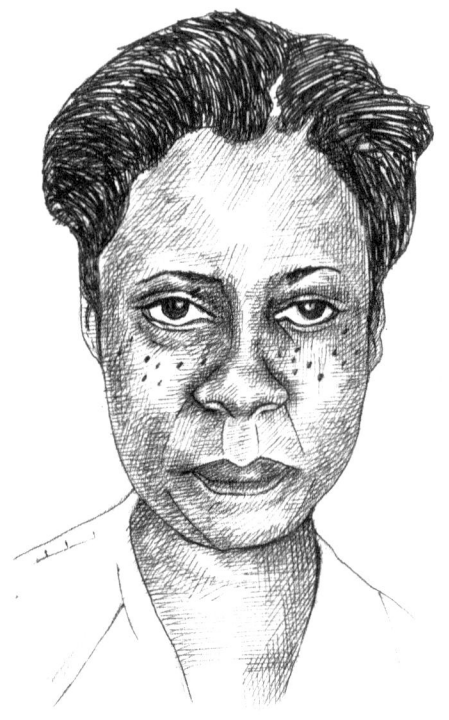

Oct. 5

Angela
Age 46
Battery on a
Law Enforcement
office, Aiding escape

P. O. B. JM
Self employed
Welding shop
Arrested
1:35 a.m.